HURTIGRUTEN

125

Published by:

Ferry Publications, PO Box 33, Ramsey, Isle of Man IM99 4LP

Tel: +44 (0) 1624 898445   Fax: +44 (0) 1624 898449   E-mail: ferrypubs@manx.net   Website: www.ferrypubs.co.uk

Acknowledgements

I am grateful to Miles Cowsill of Lily Publications for his encouragement and support, together with Daniel A. Skjeldam (CEO Hurtigruten) for the Foreword, Anne Marit Bjørnflaten (Senior Vice President Communications, Hurtigruten), Rune Thomas Ege (VP Hurtigruten Global Communications) in the writing of this book. I am also indebted in particular to Roger Gibson (proofing), Tor Arne Aasen, Mike Bent, Rory Coase, Per Eide, Jarl Hernes Gåsvær, Owe Jakob, Bård Kolltveit, Sigmund Krøvel-Velle, David Parsons, and Jan-Olav Storli for their contributions. In addition, Marilyn Gardner for the excellent maps - © Lily Publications and the Hurtigrutemuseet are also thanked for their generous input.

I have tried to ensure that all images have been correctly credited, something which is not easy in this internet age when different sources lay claim to origin. Any inaccuracies or omissions are therefore mine and I would welcome feedback so as to be able to address this in any future edition.

Finally, I need to acknowledge the support I have been given by my wife Cathy during the writing of this book, as usual patient and understanding.

Hurtigruten's classic ship *Lofoten* (1964) cruising serenely along the Raftsundet towards Trollfjord. Today, her funnel sports her original VDS livery - see page 82. *(Claus Koch/Hurtigruten)*

ISBN: 978-1-911268-15-4

Produced and designed by Ferry Publications trading as Lily Publications Ltd

PO Box 33, Ramsey, Isle of Man, British Isles, IM99 4LP

Tel: +44 (0) 1624 898446   Fax: +44 (0) 1624 898449

www.ferrypubs.co.uk   E-Mail: info@lilypublications.co.uk

Printed and bound by Gomer Press Ltd, Wales © Lily Publications 2018

Contents

Fram amidst beautiful scenery off Ilorsuit, Greenland. (*Marie-Therese Lehner-Hautle/Hurtigruten*)

Foreword

For 125 years Hurtigruten has sailed along the rugged and magnificent coastline of Norway providing guests with unique travel experiences along what is rightly known as 'the most beautiful voyage in the world'. Our very special status in Norway is based not only on stunning nature, but on the benefits that the coastal route brings as a transport artery for goods and passengers, and the value and jobs it creates by bringing travellers from all corners of the world to local communities along the coast - twice a day, every day of the year.

Hurtigruten's history stretches back to 1893, when Captain Richard With first established a year round transport link between the north and south of Norway. The route proved a communication revolution and he also quickly spotted the potential for tourism by immediately starting to market Norway internationally as a visitor destination.

125 years later, we – and small and big businesses all along the coast – still see the benefits of his pioneering spirit. We have developed the Norwegian coast as a year-round destination. Through a close partnership with a multitude of local food producers,

Daniel A. Skjeldam

The imposing hybrid explorer ship *Roald Amundsen* and sister *Fridtjof Nansen* will open up new and exciting expedition opportunities in both polar regions. *(Hurtigruten)*

The *Nordkapp* is greeted by the Northern Lights as she closes in on Tromso. *(Andreas Kalvig Anderson/Hurtigruten)*

excursion providers and others, we are able to offer our guests experiences that no one else can, bringing them in touch with the nature and culture of each local area.

In recent years Hurtigruten has markedly broadened our horizons, honouring our explorer heritage by offering breath-taking nature-based experiences to remote corners of the world, encompassing not only Norway, but also including Antarctica, some of the most remarkable parts of Svalbard, Greenland, and Iceland, and more recently Canada, the United States, the Caribbean, South America, Russia and the legendary North West Passage!

Operating in such pristine waters comes with big responsibilities which is why Hurtigruten is investing heavily in 'green technology', not only in our new hybrid powered ships Roald Amundsen and Fridtjof Nansen, but also with similar green upgrades to our current fleet, and strong focus on sustainability throughout our operation and the guest experience. This is vital to preserve environmentally sensitive areas for future generations of explorers.

I invite everyone to enjoy a voyage with Hurtigruten, either through this book or, even better, come on board for the real thing!

In the meantime, 125 years of the 'most beautiful voyage in the world' is something more than well worth celebrating!

Happy Birthday, Hurtigruten!

Daniel A. Skjeldam
CEO, Hurtigruten AS
June 2018

Introduction

Celebrations were very much the order of the day throughout 2018 for Hurtigruten, as it marked the 125th birthday of the Coastal Express service which began on 2nd July 1893. Originally it was from Trondheim to Hammerfest but by 1908 it had been extended southwards to run from Bergen and northwards to Kirkenes close to the Russian border.

The year 2018 was also cause for more celebration as in late March the Norwegian Government awarded Hurtigruten AS with the major tranche of the next Norwegian coastal service (kystruten) contract which would operate from 2021 through to 2031, thus reaffirming the company's position as a world leader in this sector of maritime transportation.

Today, Hurtigruten (literally 'fast route' which was first coined by Richard With, its founding father) is the company name, whilst the official name for the service is 'Kystruten Bergen-Kirkenes', normally translated as 'Coastal Express.

This unique heritage route offers guests breathtaking nature-based experiences whilst travelling through fantastic vistas and yet at the same time continuing its core business of serving daily the needs of the communities along Norway's coastline from Bergen to Kirkenes on what is rightly called the 'world's most beautiful voyage'.

A journey with Hurtigruten from Bergen to Kirkenes and return is along a coastline of around 2,500 nautical miles (4,000km) which has no equals with over half of the voyage north of the Arctic Circle. Depending on the time of year you can experience an endless summer's day, the magic of the Northern Lights on a clear winter's polar night and much more. Every day is different, with an ever-changing backdrop of unmatched beauty in which man's efforts to provide our energy and industrial needs somehow enable

Ports of call

Meeting up daily with another member of the fleet is always an excuse for flag waving. *(Hurtigruten)*

these edifices to appear in almost perfect harmony.

For generations, Hurtigruten has been the lifeblood of the 'long coast' carrying local passengers, cargo, post, medicines and other essential commodities and this is as important today as it ever was. It is about the people you meet on the way, travelling from port to port for business or meeting up with family and friends, the small fishing communities, delightful rural settlements as well as modern bustling towns.

It is only when you actually make such a trip that you begin to understand just how important the Coastal Express service was

Looking majestic, *Kong Harald* powers southwards to recross the Arctic Circle *(John Bryant)*

and still is to the communities who live along 'the long coast' of Northern Norway and to be able to appreciate the enterprise, experience and seamanship that was necessary to establish this link and maintain it. The arrival of the ship is the event of the day and people come down to the quayside alerted by the ship's siren and fascination of seeing the cargo doors and passenger walkway unravel almost before the vessel has kissed the quayside followed by fork lift trucks dizzily unloading and reloading cargo. From its inception with Hurtigruten has been the undisputed means of communication between small and larger communities along Norway's 'long coast' for the past 125 years. Why else would Norway name this route as Riksvei No 1 – i.e. National Highway No 1?

The past decade has seen a tremendous evolvement in Hurtigruten's modern explorer activities concept which began in 2002 using the *Nordnorge*, later joined by her sister ship *Nordkapp*, on expeditions to Antarctica. The introduction of the

purpose-built explorer ship *Fram* in 2007 saw Greenland, Iceland and Svalbard added to the itinerary. With the introduction of the *Spitsbergen* in 2016 and a further two new ships (*Roald Amundsen* and *Fridtjof Nansen*) soon to come into service, guests will have exploration opportunities which include the east coast of Canada and Newfoundland, the Caribbean and Central America as well as the whole of South America's west coast. Even further expansion is promised for 2019, with the existing coastal express service being complemented by cruises from Amsterdam and Hamburg along the Norwegian coastline and onto Svalbard, based on the legendary 'Sports Route' which Hurtigruten founder Richard With started in 1896. Another new venture will be summer cruises from Tromsø from Tromsø with calls at both Murmansk and Frans Josef's Land. Probably most exciting of all is the opportunity to experience the North West Passage to Alaska continuing southwards to Vancouver.

Being the world leader in exploration travel and particularly where climate change is already having a great impact comes with a great responsibility for preserving the natural wonders of the places served. Hurtigruten AS' stunning new ships with their hybrid technology, designed to leave the smallest eco footprint possible, are tangible proof of the company putting into practice what they believe. No small wonder that after 125 years the Hurtigruten brand is viewed with such high regard.

John Bryant

The Norwegian Postal Flag lives on! *(Hurtigruten)*

CHAPTER ONE

The World's most beautiful voyage

Before telling the story of the Hurtigruten and the coastal express route over the past 125 years let us first look at what constitutes the 'classic round voyage' to which many guests not only return but return again and again. It is a spectacular journey taking 12 days to complete with all the ports visited by night northbound being revisited by day southbound.

Day 1: Bergen founded by Olaf Kyrre in 1070 is the bustling capital of Norway's fjord district, a beautiful city set between seven mountains. Stroll around the vibrant fishmarket and onwards to the old wooden buildings of the Bryggen (a UNESCO World Heritage site) with reminders of its Hanseatic past, enjoy the wonderful view from

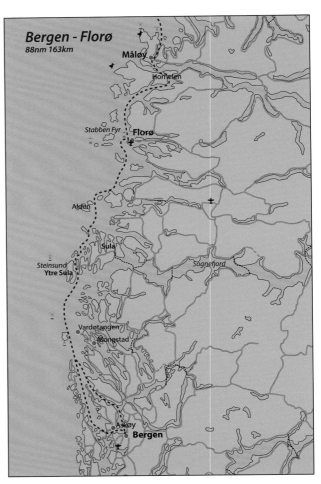

Top: Mount Fløyen provides wonderful views over Bergen. *(Tori Hogan/Hurtigruten)*

Above: The Bryggen at Bergen is a UNESCO World Heritage site. *(John Bryant)*

the top of the Fløibanen Funicular or even take the short bus ride to visit Gamle (Old) Bergen, the open air museum at Sandviken. For those with the afternoon free, then a walk along the attractive residential area of Nordnes will also afford a sight of your Hurtigruten ship arriving at the conclusion of her previous voyage.

After check in and a pre-boarding safety briefing guests have plenty of time to settle in and explore their new home. The ship will depart promptly at 20.00 (22.30 September to May) on her first leg of the journey northwards, gliding under the elegant bridge at Askøy, past Statoil's refinery at Mongstad, before rounding mainland Norway's most westerly point at Vardøtangen and sailing into the sunset off Sognefjord en route for a first call at Florø in the early hours of the following day.

Day 2: Very early risers will wake up to the breathtaking beauty of Norway as the ship, having passed the Hornelen with its 860m sea cliff, the highest in Northern Europe, then drifts under the graceful 1,224m bridge at Måløy which, if the wind is in the right direction, will resonate to a high 'c'. Having left Måløy at around 05.00 (06.30 in winter), we begin to sail towards the open waters of the Stadhavet, greeting the southbound 'express' as she passes by at close quarters. After a brief call at Torvik (opposite Ulsteinvik, where several of the current fleet were built with more to come) the ship brings travellers to Ålesund, a unique and fascinating art nouveau styled town, rebuilt after the disastrous fire of 1904. In winter, guests will have three hours to explore the town, including climbing the 418 steps to experience the fantastic view from the top of Mount Aksla. Summer visitors do not have this opportunity as the ship sails down Storfjord

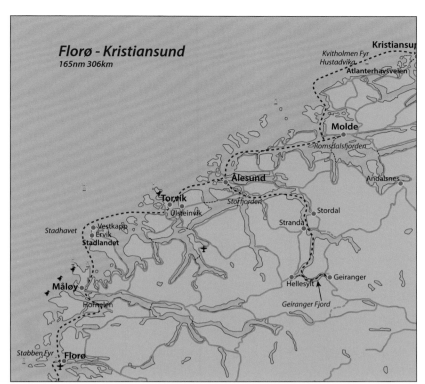

and on into the magnificent Geirangerfjord (another UNESCO World Heritage site) with its famous cascading waterfalls. Many passengers will opt for a spectacular drive back to Ålesund via the Eagle Road, a steep stretch of road up the mountain side from Geiranger through 11 hairpin bends. Others will prefer to stay on board to enjoy the return cruise. Autumn travellers are able to experience the adjacent Hjørundfjord, which cuts deep into the lush alpine Sunnmøre Alps to Urke and the town of Øye where traditionally many notable European royals spent their holidays. With everyone meeting up again at Ålesund the ship sails for an early evening call at prosperous Molde, the 'Town of the Roses', situated in the heart of 87 beautiful snow capped mountains (the Alps of

Romsdalen) and host to an International Jazz Festival each year. In summer, there is also the possibility of being able to greet another southbound Coastal Express ship.

Day 3: It will be a breakfast time arrival at 'royal' Trondheim, the first capital city of Norway, with the ship berthing behind the southbound, affording the chance to go on board and to have a look around a fleet mate. Trondheim is a jewel of a city, founded by OlafTrygvasen in AD 1000 and the starting point for Leif Erikson's journeys to the New World. Many will want to visit the Nidaros Cathedral where the new kings of Norway once were crowned, the Ringve (Music) Museum or just take a casual stroll around its charming streets, crossing the

The elegant art nouveau town of Ålesund, as seen from Mount Aksla
(Helikopter Flights)

Hurtigruten's *Polarlys* cruising along the magnificent Geirangerford
(Ørjan Bertelsen/Hurtigruten)

Beautiful Trondheim reflected in the River Nid. *(John Bryant)*

Trondheim - Rørvik
125nm 232km

Gamle Bybro (the old city bridge) to see the restored wooden buildings in Nygata and Bakklandet. The midday departure takes you past the small island of Munkholmen, its medieval monastery and 17th century fort, returning down the long Trondheimsfjorden, passing the Agdenes lighthouse and the NATO air base at Ørlandet. Once the attractive red painted Kjeungskjær Fyr (lighthouse and a family home until 1947) has been left behind, the ship navigates her way through numerous skerries and if the weather is kind, heads for the narrows of the Stokksundet, passing under the road bridge before making a spectacular and seemingly blind 90° turn to port in order to go out into the open sea of the Folda (or Folla). As you pass under the tall Nærøysund Bridge an evening call at Rørvik, capital of

Crossing the Arctic Circle is one of the highlights of the voyage. *(John Bryant)*

Not for the faint hearted - doing a backward somersault between the Goat's Horns at Svolvær. *(Jarl Hernes Gåsvær)*

Vikna, beckons as well as the opportunity to visit another southbound ship.

Day 4: This will be a busy day as you will need to be up around 07.00 to witness the crossing of the Arctic Circle at 66° 33' north; from now on in high summer you are in the 'Land of the Midnight Sun', passing the island of Vikingen with its illuminated globe on the port side and the tall mass of Hestmann Island in the background. Sometime after 08.00, the next southbound Hurtigruten will come past at speed and almost immediately afterwards our ship will stop to allow guests to board the tender to visit the famous Svartisen Glacier and later on experience the sight of the spectacular Saltstraumen tidal current which can flow at amazing speed (22 knots/40km per hour!). Ørnes is a pretty little settlement at which a brief call is made, surrounded by mountains, and then it is on to Bodø, a town well worth exploring with its modern cathedral and Nordland Museum. It also boasts one of Norway's largest airports, a combined civil and military base, which in the U2 Cold War days was of significant importance.

The mid afternoon departure takes the ship past the island of Landegøde which probably has the most photographed lighthouse in the country and then across the Vestfjord to the Lofotens *(see also Harstad-Bodø Map for Day 9)*. The forbidding 100km Lofoten mountain wall can be seen from a long way out, as the ship calls first at Stamsund where, in summer, you can go off on a 'Viking Feast' experience. The ship continues its journey parallel to the 'wall', passing the southbound 'express' somewhere off Henningsvær, its cliffs teeming with sea birds. An evening call at the artists' paradise of Svolvær provides the opportunity to have a gentle stroll up to the

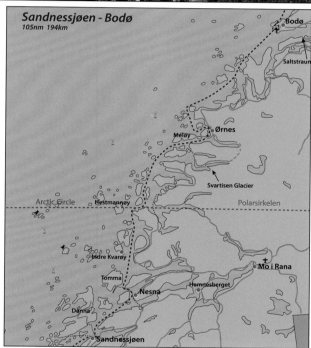

local church, get close up views of the stock-fish drying racks and the traditional red painted fishermen's cabins known as rorbuer, as well as gazing from afar at the famous Svolværgeita (Goat Mountain) with its twin peaks, which intrepid adventurers are dared to leap across.

The day will end with the ship traversing the Raftsundet, a 20km channel which separates Lofoten from Vesterålen. If conditions are right, then towards midnight, the ship will sail into Trollfjord, the sight of the famous battle in 1880 between the traditional sailboat fishermen and the new steam powered trawlers. At the end of the narrow fjord, the ship will turn on its axis, with seemingly little room to spare, before continuing its journey.

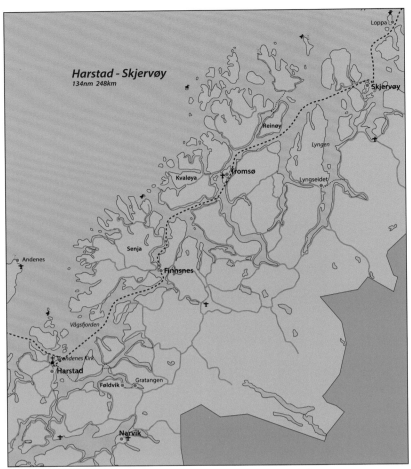

Harstad - Skjervøy
134nm 248km

Day 5: Guests will wake up to an early morning arrival at and departure from Harstad, the main town for Norway's fourth largest island, Hinnøy. The southbound vessel will arrive just as our ship gets underway and after a few minutes Trondenes Church, the oldest stone church in Norway dating from 1250, will be passed. The ship sails across Vagsfjord, past the great island of Senja, with its diverse countryside of farmland, pine trees and plunging peaks, calling at Finnsnes, a busy settlement dominated by the magnificent 1,220m Gisund Bridge which links the island to the mainland. It is an afternoon arrival at Tromsø, the 'Gateway to the Arctic', known also as the 'Paris of the North'. Tromsø is a thriving town of 60,000 inhabitants with an excellent shopping centre, its harbour dominated by the bridge which takes you across to the Arctic Cathedral with its wonderful stained glass capturing the light. A number of excursions are on offer here including a tour around Tromsø, or you can take the cable car up the Fjellheisen for stunning views across the city. In winter, you have the opportunity to go dog sledging.

The iconic Arctic Cathedral at Tromsø. *(Nordic Experience)*

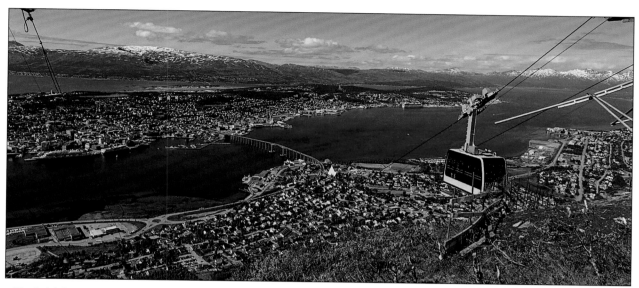

Wonderful vistas can be had from the cable car station overlooking Tromsø. *(Ørjan Bertelsen/Hurtigruten)*

The ship then heads north for the old trading post of Skjervøy, founded in 1622, passing the soaring slopes of the daunting Lyngen Alps, a mountaineer's paradise. In the winter months if conditions are right from now on you have a good chance of observing the Northern Lights. The next southbound Coastal Express ship will pass us mid evening.

Day 6: Whilst most people will still be asleep when the ship calls at Hammerfest early that morning, it is a day of expectant excitement as we head for Honningsvåg and Nordkapp (North Cape) passing a southbound ship, just prior to a call at Havøysund, dominated by its large wind farm and do look out for the painted stone troll opposite

the ship's berth. Finnmark's landscape is austere in its beauty, teeming with birdlife; watch out for puffins and gannets along the cliffs. After an early lunchtime arrival at Honningsvåg the ship will empty as nearly everyone takes the coach to Nordkapp, almost, but not quite (that's at Knivskjellodden just to the west), the most northerly point of mainland Europe at 71° 10' 21"N and just 2,000km from the North Pole. It is the excursion of the voyage with an opportunity in summer to visit a Sami encampment on the way. Some will opt to visit the Gjesvaer Bird Sanctuary to witness the thousands of seabirds which nest there, including puffins, kittiwakes, guillemots and sea eagles. For those who like a quieter time, a stroll around Honningsvåg can be very rewarding, remembering that the

The stunning Northern Lights over Arnøya, Skjervøy. *(Jan R Olsen/Hurtigruten)*

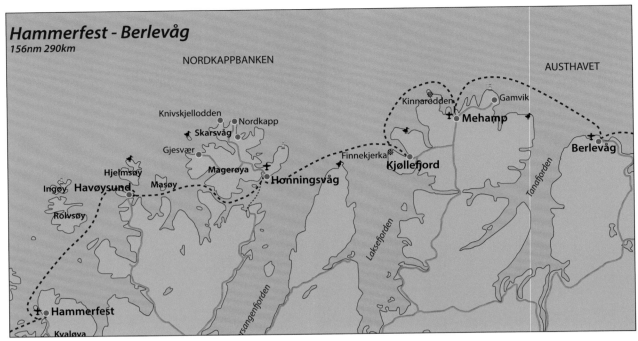

Hammerfest - Berlevåg
156nm 290km

Top: Sunset at Nordkapp. *(Magdalena Liebing/Hurtigruten)*

Above: Finnjerka (the Cathedral) is a rock formation near Kjølleford and is a Sami sacred place. *(John Bryant)*

only building left standing at the end of the Second World War was the local church.

Our ship then heads eastwards to Kjøllefjord and home of the giant king crab, passing the strange rock formation known as the Finnkjerka (Cathedral) which once was a Sami sacrificial site. Calls at the pretty fishing ports of Mehamn (average summer temperatures are never higher than 10°C, so officially it doesn't qualify as having a summer) and Berlevåg help one to appreciate the isolation of this part of Northern Norway and of the importance of the service to the local communities. Late evening at Berlevåg there is usually a very loud and raucous exchange between the crews of the two passing Coastal Express ships as they try to outdo each other, making it a great end to a long and exciting day.

Day 7: By the time Vadsø (in Varangerfjord) is reached around 07.30 the next morning we are very much further south and east than yesterday, in fact as far east as St Petersburg and Istanbul. Vadsø has strong Finnish connections, with the language still taught in the local schools, and was also once an important 'pomor' trading centre between Russia and Norway. Sea eagles and hooded crows are frequently sighted, but notice how stunted the vegetation has become. To the east of the berth is the preserved mooring mast constructed for the airship 'Norge' flown by Roald Amundsen in 1926 and Umberto Nobile two years later. Kirkenes, an important fishing and ship repair port (and formerly with an extensive iron ore mining industry) is reached around 09.00, the end of the journey for some. Many will take advantage of the excellent excursions on offer, visiting a snow hotel, dog sledging or a riverboat safari. Others will take a tour to the Russian border just 10 kilometres away or just

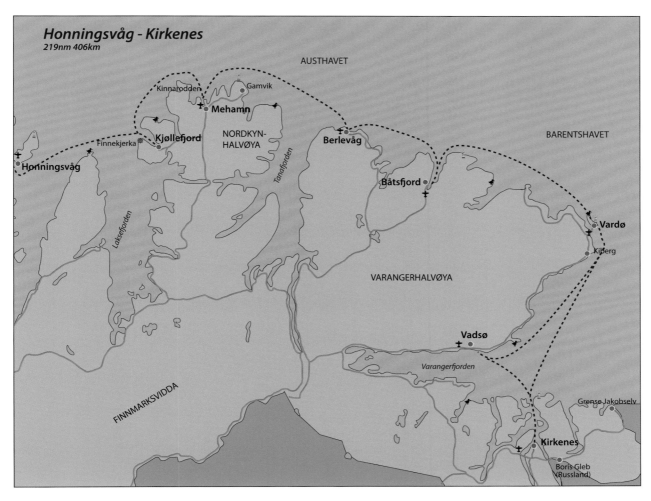

Honningsvåg - Kirkenes
219nm 406km

enjoy the 20-minute walk into town.

Three hours later and the ship begins to retrace her path to reach Vardø (note the NATO early warning installations) during the late afternoon. The old fort built in 1737 (a popular visit) is still part of the military, guarded by one officer and four men. It also has the most cared for tree in Norway, a rowan which is wrapped up by the soldiers in October and only unpacked in April. Alternatively, visit the distinctive contemporary church where you will get a warm welcome. Båtsfjord is the next port of call with a sheltered harbour, well used by both local and visiting fishing trawlers. Båtsfjord's remoteness ensured that it was the only large community not to be razed to the ground by the German retreat from Finnmark in 1944.

Kirkenes Church; note the road signs are in both Norwegian and Russian. *(John Bryant)*

Signpost at Kirkenes, it's a long way to anywhere. *(John Bryant)*

Vardøhus Fort, Vardø, built in the 18th century and still manned, note the three NATO early warning domes in the background. *(John Bryant)*

The view over Hammerfest from Mount Salen. *(Reinhard Gerwin /Hurtigruten)*

In late evening, the ship sails on to meet the northbound 'express' off Berlevåg for a noisy repeat performance from the rival crews. Until 1973 embarkation and disembarkation was always by tender until two breakwaters were constructed with massive 15 tonne tetrapod blocks which finally made the harbour a safe haven.

Day 8: Insomniacs may have risen early to take the excursion from Honningsvåg in order to have breakfast at Nordkapp. Having passed another northbound Coastal Express around 09.00 near Havøysund, the day's highlights will include an extended stop at Hammerfest, officially the world's most northerly town (and the first Norwegian town to have electric street lighting and its own power station), with the opportunity to do some shopping, visit the Polar Bear Club or pause for thought in one or both of its lovely modern churches. In summer, those who take the zig zag path behind the town to the top will be rewarded with stunning views across the whole area. The gas flare from the giant Melkøy oil and gas terminal can be seen from miles around. Øksfjord is visited mid afternoon and is an isolated but thriving community with the Øksfjordjøkulen Glacier opposite. This calves into the sea at Jøkelfjorden, just around the corner. There is another brief evening stop at Skjervøy, the pretty little settlement with its church dating from 1728, surrounded by mountain peaks. During April and May, as part of Hurtigruten's 'The Arctic Awakening', ships make another diversion this time into Lyngenfjord with its sweeping views of the 'Kvænangtindan' mountain range and Lyngen Alps. Tromsø is reached very late in the evening (having passed the northbound ship around 21.00) there you can experience a midnight concert at the Arctic Cathedral with its 140 m² glass mosaic, the largest in Europe, or in summer just stroll around the still busy city in the 24 hour daylight.

Day 9: In great contrast to the rugged brooding mountains of Finnmark, early morning finds the ship back in beautiful Hinnøya arriving at Harstad just in time to

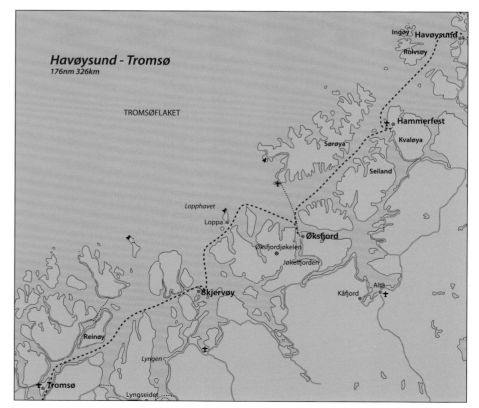

Havøysund - Tromsø
176nm 326km

TROMSØFLAKET

Ingøy Havøysund
Rolvsøy

Hammerfest
Sørøya Kvaløya

Seiland

Lopphavet
Loppa
Øksfjord
Øksfjordjøkelen
Jøkelfjorden

Skjervøy

Kåfjord Alta

Reinøy

Lyngen

Tromsø
Lyngseidet

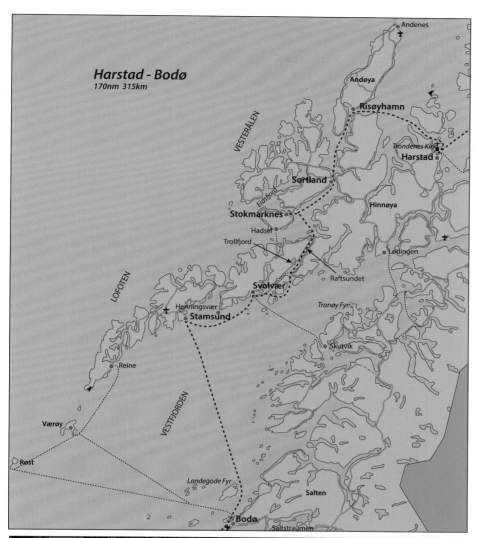

Harstad - Bodø
170nm 315km

see the northbound vessel depart at 07.45. This will be the day when the ship will carefully negotiate the shallow waters of the man-made Risøyrenna Channel, with the sand banks visible through the clear green water, pausing for a brief stop at Risøyhamn, nestling in the shadow of the modern bridge which connects Hinnøya with Andøya. You will then pass through the stunning scenery of the islands of Vesterålen, berthing at Sortland, the home of Norway's North Atlantic Coastguard Patrol Fleet, noting just how many shades of blue have been used to paint the houses. Later on the ship will arrive at Stokmarknes, the spiritual home of Hurtigruten, where Richard With, the founder, was based. Here is the Hurtigruten Museum, a major visitor attraction, an integral part of which is the previous *Finnmarken* (1956–1993) high and dry out of the water and by

A night time view from the outside of the magnificent altar window of Tromsø's Arctic Cathedral. *(Niel Goslett/Hurtigruten)*

It looks like a very tight squeeze as **Nordnorge** negotiates Trollfjord. *(John Bryant)*

Boreal's fastcraft **Falkefjell** races past Norway's most northerly medieval stone church at Trondenes, Harstad en route to Tromsø. *(John Bryant)*

The beautiful town of Svolvær captured as the moon rises over the harbour. *(Miles Cowsill)*

far Norway's largest museum exhibit. By the end of 2019 the ship will be enclosed in a futuristic glazed structure ensuring her permanent preservation.   Mid afternoon sees the ship travelling along the spectacular Raftsundet to re-enter Trollfjord, (just as impressive in daylight as at night). Some guests will transfer to an excursion boat which precedes the ship into the fjord and then stays on in order to witness the sea eagles feeding. After a return call at Svolvær and the opportunity to take a coach excursion around the Lofoten Islands, the ship will cruise along the Lofoten Wall, passing the northbound Hurtigruten before a last call of the day at Stamsund.

Day 10: Following a breakfast time stop at the attractive settlement of Ørnes *(see also Sandnessjøen – Bodø Map for Day 4)*, the ship will glide southwards in crystalline waters, past lush agricultural fields, through the islands and skerries, meeting up with the next northbound vessel before re-crossing the Arctic Circle. Nesna, a very pretty village with a stunning mountain backdrop, is visited briefly during the late morning and has an important direct road link to the industrial town of Mo i Rana. The ship will berth at both Sandnessjøen and Brønnøysund, each framed by attractive bridges linking the islands, the former being an important shipbuilding and

The **Finnmarken** (1956) is an integral part of the Hurtigruten Museum, Stokmarknes; **Polarlys** berthed in the background. *(Aslak Tonrud/Hurtigruten)*

Midnight in high summer as *Midnatsol* approaches Brønnøysund. *(Hans-Joacim Edel)*

repair centre serving the offshore oil and gas industry. Between the two ports are the famous Seven Sisters mountain peaks of Helgeland where, according to Norwegian folklore, trolls are turned into stone. Brønnøysund is a fine town, but for most travellers the real attraction is when the ship takes a wide westerly arc in order to get a good view of Torghatten Mountain with its hole (160m long x 30m high and 15m wide) right through the middle; a troll tale claims that it was caused when the local hero Hestmann fired his arrow through the Brønnøy king's hat, turning him to stone. Tonight is also the occasion when the evening meal is designated as the 'Captain's Dinner' and gives an opportunity for guests to thank the crew for their wonderful service. A late evening arrival at Rørvik offers the chance to visit a third member of the fleet at the end of a busy day.

Day 11: Back in Trondheim again, a shorter stay southbound (until 10.00) but still enough time to revisit the city or to have a look around the next northbound vessel. Some will take the Dovrebanen (train) through magnificent Norwegian countryside to end their journey at Oslo. The ship retraces her path along the fjord and then westwards through the channel which separates the islands of Hitra (the island of deer) and Smøla from the mainland. It will be over six hours before Kristiansund is reached, an attractive town in a lovely setting with its three islands linked by bridges, famous as far back as 1691 as the 'klippfisk' (dried salted cod) capital of

Sandnessjøen - Rørvik
82nm 152km

Dønna

Sandnessjøen

Seven Sisters

Alstahaug

Mosjøen

Vega

Brønnøysund

Torghatten

Leka

Vikna Rørvik

Hurtigruten's **Nordlys** passes the iconic Torghatten mountain near Brønnøysund. *(Author's Collection)*

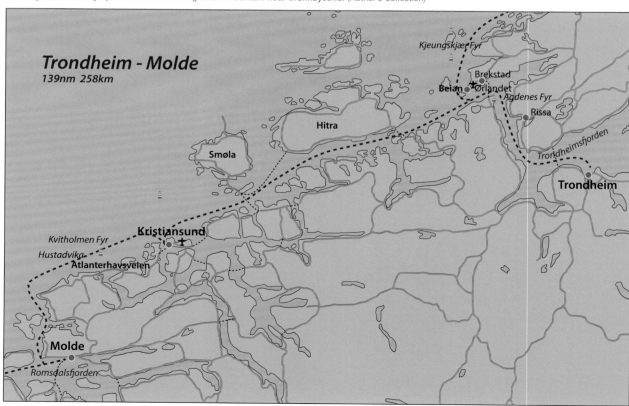

Trondheim - Molde
139nm 258km

The spectacular 8km Atlantic Highway, which runs south of Kristiansund. *(Atlanterhavsveien)*

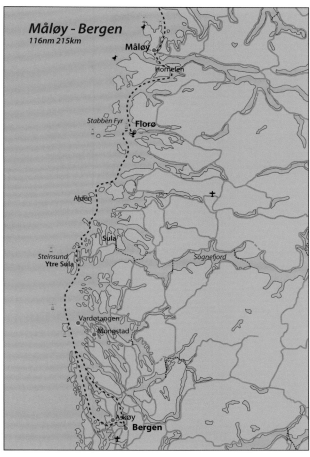

Norway. It is a town made prosperous today by the offshore oil and gas industry.

There is also an opportunity to go on a sightseeing tour of Kristiansund prior to experiencing the full length of the Atlanterhavsveien (Atlantic Road), before rejoining the ship at Molde. In the summer months at Molde you will also meet up with the northbound Coastal Express.

Day 12: All too quickly it is the final day of the voyage. The early risers may see the northbound 'express' as we approach Måløy. Florø, a large fishing town and oil industry supply base, is Norway's most westerly based town and the final stop before Bergen. Yet still ahead lies mile after mile of spectacular scenery, the extreme narrows to be negotiated at Steinsundet, crossing the mouth of Sognefjord before gliding serenely through the archipelago on the approaches to Bergen. Once Statoil's refinery at Mongstad is sighted, the journey is almost over. Whilst arrival at Bergen is around 14.30, many will be in no spiritual hurry to leave the ship which has been their home for the past eleven days. Some guests will stay on in Bergen for another day. For whatever reason people have travelled, whether it was for the scenery, the wildlife, the camaraderie or just relaxation, it will have been a truly memorable experience. For it is 'the world's most beautiful voyage'.

The 1867 built wooden Stabben Lighthouse guards the approaches to Florø. *(Author's Collection)*

The *Polarlys* berthed at the Hurtigruten Terminal, Bergen. *(Rory Coase/Ships in Bergen)*

CHAPTER TWO

Beginnings

Man has travelled and traded up and down the 'long coast' of Norway with wares of dried fish, cured meats and animal skins for well over a millennium. The traditional form of trading ship was a 'jekt', a small vessel with one or two sails, around 100 feet in length and capable of carrying around 40 tons of cargo. A voyage south to Bergen was not easy as there were no navigational aids to guide them, therefore knowledge of the sea routes was passed down from one generation to another. Sailing in darkness was extremely dangerous and so comparatively little business was done outside of the summer season.

Even though in 1647 the Norwegian Government's General Auditor, Henrik Morian, had begun to establish a national postal network, it was overland and journey times were, to say the least, unpredictable. By the beginning of the eighteenth century the government, seeing the need to get important documents and mail to the regional administrations more efficiently, had built up a chain of designated villages roughly a day's sailing apart to act as refuges and trading posts. Each village was required to provide a least one inn (gjestgiveri) where travellers could stay overnight.

At the turn of the nineteenth century a båtpost (postal boat) service was introduced from Trondheim to Bodø, Tromsø and Alta. These boats were in reality little more than large rowing boats with a small sail, crewed by teams of 4 rowers. Not surprisingly, post would still take an inordinate time to arrive, up to three weeks to reach Tromsø and anything up to five months if it were ever to reach Hammerfest!

The introduction of the steamship was to change everything when, in 1827, two wooden hulled paddle steamers were ordered by the Norwegian Government to carry mails from Christiania (Oslo) to Kristiansand, Gothenburg and Copenhagen. Despite being of only 100 feet in length and a service speed of 7 knots both the *Constitutionen* (250 gross tons) and *Prinds Carl* (375 gross tons) were immediately successful. As steamship operations elsewhere demonstrated their worth it increased the pressure on the Storting (Norwegian Parliament) to provide a passenger and mail service between Trondheim and Hammerfest. In 1836 the Storting allocated 15,000 speciedalers (the currency at that time) annually for three years to cover the cost of setting up and maintaining this service.

The first organised coastal route to north Norway began on 14th March 1838 using the diminutive paddle steamship *Prinds Gustav* (215 gross tons) which had a service speed of 8 knots. Initially she sailed between Trondheim and Tromsø and on her first voyage carried just 7 passengers. Her passenger accommodation was spartan with dormitory type cabins and she had almost no space for

A traditional jekt underway off Trondheim circa 1905. *(Anders Beer Wilse)*

The diminutive båtpost (postal boat), soon to be superceded by the paddle steamer. *(Mike Bent)*

An engraving by Christian Tønsberg of the *Constitutionen* at Arendal in 1848. *(Author's Collection)*

cargo. By 1845 the Storting had expanded their coastal steamer service to link Christiania with Kristiansand (*Prinds Carl*), Kristiansand to Trondheim (*Nordcap*) and Trondheim to Tromsø, extended to Hammerfest in the summer months (*Prinds Gustav*).

As demands grew and routes were further expanded within a short space of time the Norwegian Post Office had 11 vessels on its books of which 9 were needed at any one time. As these ships began to show their age, several private shipping companies introduced competing passenger and cargo services (albeit without mail) with far better appointed ships.

In 1857 the Storting, bowing to increasing pressure, agreed to private companies being allowed to carry mail and receiving a state subsidy for doing so. Two of these companies, Det Bergenske Dampskibsselskab (BDS) and Det Nordenfjeldske Dampskibsselskab (NFDS) became the major players in this 'kombinerte (passenger/mail/cargo) enterprise and effectively creamed off the market before then entering into a joint tariff system.

There were the inevitable rumblings over the standards of the subsidised service, especially when in 1875, the two companies asked for and received an increase in subsidy to 90,000 speciedalers per annum (replaced later that year by the krone; 4 kroner = 1 speciedaler). In 1880, whilst 260,000 kroner per annum was available for mail services between Bergen, Trondheim, Hammerfest and Vadsø, only one NFDS ship's master was prepared to venture beyond Hammerfest in the winter.

Further revenue earnings came in the form of increased tourism with both BDS and NFDS promoting summer cruises from Trondheim to Nordkapp, later extended to and from Bergen, where the majority of the estimated 14,000 foreign tourists each year would arrive.

A number of these steamers led dual roles which continued right up to the onset of the First World War, whereby each spring, having spent the winter primarily as black hulled cargo carriers, they were transformed into cruise ships with white hulls and superstructure, canvas dodgers along the deck rails and large awnings to protect passengers from the weather. Skylights replaced cargo hatch covers and portable cabins were erected in the holds.

The rich herring fisheries industry of the Vesterålen and Lofoten Islands had, as early as the 1860s, highlighted the need for better

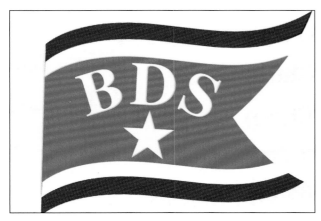

House flag of BDS (Det Bergen Dampskibsselskab) – Bergen Steamship Company

Trondheim based NFDS' (Det Nordenfjeldske Dampskibsselskab) house flag

Richard With, founder of Hurtigruten in 1893.

Richard With's **Arendal** after her rebuilding, later renamed **Vesteraalen** in 1881.

transport services in order to distribute their catch more efficiently. Growing dissatisfaction eventually led Captain Richard With to form, on 10th November 1881, the Det Vesteraalens Dampskibsselskab (Steamship Company), based at Stokmarknes, the municipal capital of Vesteraalen.

Det Vesteraalens Dampskibsselskab (VDS) raised 4,000 kroner to purchase the steamship *Arendal* which they renamed *Vesteraalen*. Built in Gothenburg in 1865, the vessel had berths for 18 passengers, a speed of 10 knots and was reinforced for service in ice conditions, in which sailing ships could not easily operate. She was a modern vessel for her time and became a successful investment for the company, in particular during the winter season.

The *Vesteraalen,* with Richard With as Master, went into direct competition with BDS and the NFDS on the route between Bergen and Vesterålen. Her main cargo was transporting the local herring southwards to Bergen. Around this time the largest ever herring

catch in the world was recorded, it was said to be so great that the entire Eidsfjord (adjacent to Stokmarknes) was blocked until the herring could be landed. Over 40,000 barrels were salted but much was sadly left to rot as they didn't have the capacity to process all the fish.

The *Vesteraalen's* success resulted in the construction in 1884 of the *Lofoten* for the fledgling company. Delivered from Akers Mek Verkstad, Christiania (Oslo) she was luxuriously fitted out, even boasting a piano in the ladies' lounge. It was not all plain sailing for VDS as on 9th September 1885, the *Lofoten* ran aground and sank off Haugnes, Vesterålen. There was an exceptionally low tide and the

A rare image of VDS' **Lofoten** (1884), well laden as she departs Tromsø. *(Tromsø Museet)*

August Kreigsman Gran, National Steamship Advisor for Norway 1891 and instigator of the Coastal Express. *(DSD)*

ship appeared to have struck an unmarked reef. The *Lofoten* was not return to service until the following April. After this the two ships settled down to provide a weekly service to Bergen carrying both passengers and cargo. Later on when the new *Vesteraalen* was out of service for scheduled maintenance work the *Lofoten* acted as a relief ship from 1893 until 1903. Sadly, the ship was destroyed by fire in August 1912.

By 1890 the *Vesteraalen* was becoming a victim of her own success as she was now far too small for the traffic on offer. Finding nothing suitable in the second hand tonnage market, VDS ordered the construction of a new and larger triple expansion engined vessel, again from Akers Mek. Costing 235,000 kroner the ship, a combined passenger and cargo vessel with an insulated cold room for the carriage of fish, was delivered in January 1891. As built, she had a greater cargo capacity in comparison to other ships plying the same trade, being designed specifically for VDS's regular services between Tromsø and Bergen, where freight was of greater importance than passengers or mail.

Measuring 623 gross tons, with a service speed of 10 knots, the ship had a passenger certificate for 200 in three classes, with sleeping accommodation for 25 passengers in 1st class and for 15 passengers in 2nd class, boasting electric lighting throughout. She too was named *Vesteraalen.*

The first *Vesteraalen*, which did not see Hurtigruten service, was sold to Erik Rusten (Bergen), who renamed her *Nordfjord* prior to selling her on to Vestenfjeldske, Bergen in 1891. She had a long career under several more owners and was even converted into a diesel powered coaster in 1947, before finally being scrapped at Stavanger in 1971 at the grand old age of 106!

THE FIRST TWENTY FIVE YEARS - THE COASTAL EXPRESS TAKES SHAPE

In 1891, August Kreigsman Gran, national steamship advisor for Norway, began to actively promote the idea of an express boat service between Trondheim and Hammerfest. There were a number of factors behind this submission. The growth of the 'kombinerte' (cargo/passenger/mail) services meant that there were now 58 ports between Bergen and Hammerfest (48 of which were north of Trondheim) and as a consequence travel was very slow as operators wanted to call at as many ports as possible in order to maximise their profits. Government administrators, merchants and travellers needed something quicker and began to vent their frustration. The opening of the Christiania (Oslo) to Trondheim Railway in 1880 meant that the two cities were now only 12 hours apart and travellers wanted to see this improvement translated further north. For freight businesses the protracted sailing times also tended to reduce the value of perishable goods, particularly fish. By limiting the calls to 9 intermediate ports it was felt that a 'coastal express' service could succeed.

Anders Holte, Richard With's pilot and navigator who helped chart the route to Hammerfest.

Det Nordenfjeldske Dampskibsselskab (NFDS) and Det Bergenske Dampskibsselskab (BDS) were offered the route by Gran, but turned it down as sailing safely during darkness in stormy waters was still considered impossible. At that time only two marine charts existed and there were only 28 lighthouses north of Trondheim.

It was left to Det Vesteraalens Dampskibsselskab (VDS), still a small shipping company, to take up the challenge. Captain Richard With had, with his pilot, Anders Holte, kept accurate records of courses, speeds and times taken to sail the route and was confident that such a service was viable. When it became clear that the *Vesteraalen* was going to serve on the extended route, she was sent to Bergen for a hasty rebuild with additional cabins and a spacious mailroom, raising her tonnage to 623 gross tons.

On 18th May 1893, the Government signed a four-year contract with the company to support a year-round weekly sailing between Trondheim and Tromsø, extended to Hammerfest during the summer. For this VDS would receive an annual state aid of 70,000 kroner. Under the terms of the contract the company were obliged to provide at least 40 first class sleeping berths (30 in winter) together with 16 second class and 50 third class berths on each service, as well as having a second steamer ready in reserve at all times.

On 2nd July 1893 the new *Vesteraalen,* with Captain Richard With as master and Hans Hveding Berg Jensen as pilot, left just after 08.00 on her first round-trip journey from the Brattøra Quay, Trondheim for Hammerfest, with intermediate calls at Rørvik, Brønnøysund, Sandnessjøen, Bodø, Svolvær, Lødingen, Harstad, Tromsø and Skjervøy. On board were some 60 passengers, mainly guests invited by the company. The ship arrived at Svolvær (Lofotens)

VDS' *Vesteraalen* at Bodø on her inaugural voyage in July 1893, embarking passengers by tender. *(VDS/Hurtigrutemuseet)*

on Monday 3rd July just before 20.00 (after 35½ hours) reaching her northbound destination of Hammerfest on Wednesday 5th July at 03.30, some thirty minutes ahead of schedule. The vessel had completed the northbound leg between Trondheim and Hammerfest in a total of 67 hours.

The 'express' had been born! It transformed expectations and communications completely and mail could now be received within a few days. Initially, they sailed at night only during the summer, when it remains light for most of the time. Soon, with his accurate notes on courses, speeds and times, Captain Richard With began sailing in the dark throughout the year. Admittedly, it was still not always easy to keep time and delays were frequently recorded.

The *Vesteraalen* was to have an exceptionally long career. Replaced by the new *Lofoten* in 1932, she acted in a relief capacity

The *Vesteraalen*'s crew pose for the camera, dated 1893. *(Hurtigrutemuseet)*

BDS' *Sirius* was the company's first ship on the service and is seen prior to this at Molde in 1890; her career was to last 55 years. *(Axel Lindahl/Norwegian Museum of Cultural History)*

NFDS' elegant *Olaf Kyrre* (1886) is photographed departing Trondheim. *(Anders Beer Wilse/Norwegian Maritime Museum)*

before being leased to Narvik Dampskibsselskap for their services between Narvik and Trondheim. She remained active until 1941 when on 17th October she was torpedoed and sunk off Øksfjord by the Russian Submarine SHCH-402 with the loss of 60 lives.

This modest beginning heralded a new era for the remote coastal communities, providing business and inhabitants with a ready means of transport between the cities and ultimately to the outside world. During the first few years of operation mail and passengers provided the main income on the Coastal Express, but slowly the cargo element was to become more and more prominent as the original 'kombinerte' (passenger/mail/cargo) coastal services began to suffer a long slow demise.

DOUBLING UP......

The original proposals were for a twice-weekly Coastal Express and in 1894 both NFDS and BDS were again approached to see if they might now participate. Their positive response was met with some alarm by VDS who felt that this would be a competing service

and not a complementary one. However, common sense prevailed, firstly by writing in a clause preventing unfair competition and secondly by extending VDS' contract until 30th June 1898. BDS and NFDS agreed to share their part of the contract by alternating their ships on the route each year. The former introduced the nine-year old *Sirius* (1894) on 3rd July 1894 and in the following year it was the turn of the *Olaf Kyrre* (1886) to come onto the service for NFDS. Departures from the Brattøra Quay, Trondheim, were every Thursday at 08.00, timed to link up with the overnight train from Christiania whilst the *Vesteraalen* had the departure on Sundays.

Whilst the *Sirius* was to have a career lasting 55 years, which only came to an end in May 1940 when she was sunk by German aircraft, the *Olav Kyrre's* career was much shorter, as in dense fog on 10th July 1909, whilst crossing the Hustadvika en route from Molde to Kristiansund, she became stranded on rocks and sank. Fortunately the steamship *Mercur* was able to rescue all the passengers and crew.

Up to now none of the three ships on the route had been purpose

Another fine study by Anders Beer Wilse in 1906 of *Olaf Kyrre*'s master on the port bridge wing. *(Norwegian Maritime Museum)*

NFDS' 1895 ship *Erling Jarl* departing Tromsø. *(Norwegian Maritime Museum)*

A Mittet postcard for NFDS of *Erling Jarl*; note that her cargo holds are forward which when fully laden caused the bow to dig deep into the water when at speed.

built, but this changed with the arrival of the *Erling Jarl* delivered from Trondheim Mek to NFDS on 9th December 1895. Unlike the usual coastal steamer ships of the time, the cargo holds were set forward in front of the boiler room, with the lounges and cabins on the main deck and a continuous promenade deck above. The accommodation was divided into three classes, with 1st class aft, 2nd class amidships and 3rd class towards the bow. With the holds situated forward, the ship had a tendency to dip its bow deep into the water when running at full speed.

The sharing arrangement between NFDS and BDS meant that ships would only normally serve on the Coastal Express for one year at a time. Thus whilst the *Erling Jarl* was the first purpose-built ship for the route, she needed to find other employment after 1st July

1896 as the *Jupiter* from BDS would take over for the next 12 months; paradoxically their oldest vessel. As new, the *Jupiter* had an elegant cut bow and three masts, schooner rigged, but also a huge appetite for coal, consuming some 10 barrels an hour at 12 knots! The *Erling Jarl* was put on to the weekly Trondheim – Bergen tourist service returning in the summer of 1897 for another 12-month spell on the Coastal Express.

Increasing pressure from the important fishing ports of Kristiansund and Molde had resulted in a new weekly round trip between Bergen and Tromsø as from 1898, the contract being again awarded to BDS and NFDS, with the former being responsible for the first year. BDS introduced their comparatively 'new' 24-year old *Orion* (1874); a ship which had a reputation for being accident

A modern painting by Olav Johannessen of the *Orion* on fire off Båtsfjord in 1903. *(Hurtigrutemuseet)*

Smoking furiously BDS' *Capella* (1885) is captured here at full speed *(Hurtigwiki.de)*

One of the few known images of the ill fated *Astræa* which dated from 1900. *(Author's Collection)*

Another Anders Beer Wilse image, this time of *Kong Halfdan* at Trondheim. *(Norwegian Maritime Museum)*

prone, sinking off Meløy near Ørnes in 1874 and then having her engine explode during testing after a refit in 1889. From July 1898 she sailed opposite the *Vesteraalen* until the October, when Bergen became the southernmost port on the route. NFDS's *Erling Jarl* returned to the route yet again and was joined by the BDS ship *Capella*.

However, accidents continued to haunt the *Orion* as on 12th December 1903 when eastbound off Båtsfjord, fire broke out on board after an oil lamp tipped over in the midships 2nd class accommodation. The fire spread rapidly and seven of the crew perished in the flames, while the others abandoned ship. The burnt-out wreck was then towed to Vardø where her relatively new triple expansion engine and boilers were salvaged, later to be installed in the new coastal steamer ship *Lyra* (1905).

This contract also expanded the route with a separate connection between Tromsø and Vardø, NFDS sending their *Kong Halfdan* (1874) north for the first year. The route along the exposed coast of Finnmark with its unprotected ports made for greater demands on both ships and seamanship. In the winter it was a weekly round trip service from Tromsø to Vardø but in the summer it became twice weekly from Vardø to Hammerfest. In July 1899, as per the contract

agreement the *Kong Halfdan* was replaced by the *Orion*, but sailed again in 12-month periods between July 1900 and 1904.

Southwards, further extensions to Bergen were proposed, with BDS suggesting that in order to save time, their recently introduced *Capella* (1885) should call at Beian, at the mouth of Trondheimsfjorden, where a local steamer service would provide a connection for Trondheim. This prompted a great deal of protest, in particular from NFDS as they thought the proposal might marginalise Trondheim and threatened to break off cooperation. BDS relented, so that as from 5th April 1899 Trondheim was to have three weekly Coastal Express departures to Hammerfest every Wednesday, Friday and Sunday. The *Vesteraalen* had the Sunday departure, while the *Erling Jarl*, *Orion* and *Capella* retained the other round trips.

In 1899, BDS ordered another Coastal Express steamer from Akers Mek, Christiania, for delivery in 1900. Costing some 458,000 kroner, the *Astræa* was slightly larger than the *Erling Jarl* but had the more conventional arrangement of cargo space both fore and aft of the engine room. Her razor sharp lines gave an impression of both speed and strength. Indeed this was true as her large and fuel thirsty triple expansion engine could help to her to achieve 14.25 knots. She was really a wolf in sheep's clothing being designed to double

A white hulled *Haakon Adelstein* (possibly on royal family duty) backs away from her berth at Trondheim. *(Hurtigrutemuseet)*

A BDS image of a well patronised *Lyra* whose engines were rescued from the *Orion* which had been scrapped after her fire in 1903.

33

A popular Mittet postcard of VDS' 1909 ship *Richard With* at the Festingskaien (Fortress Quay), Bergen. *(Author's Collection)*

up as an auxiliary cruiser in the event of mobilisation. This was a very real scenario, as at that time tensions between Norway and Sweden over sovereignty were beginning to become rather heated. On board she had a 120mm cannon on the foredeck, with six 76 mm and six 47mm guns placed elsewhere.

The *Astræa* was to become the first ship to be lost whilst on Coastal Express duties, grounding on 5th January 1910, just northeast of the Stabben Lighthouse, near Florø. Fortunately all the passengers and mail were saved, but the ship sank in shallow water. She was raised but following an inspection was scrapped.

Rather strangely in 1902 NFDS decided to replace the *Erling Jarl* and *Olaf Kyrre* with one of its oldest ships, the *Haakon Adalstein* (1873). Later, in the spring of both 1905 and 1907 the ship replaced the *Kong Halfdan* on the Finnmark leg of the Coastal Express and was destined to have a surprisingly long service life. The vessel undertook valuable supply work during the Second World War and indeed in November 1945 actually returned to Coastal Express service between Tromsø and Kirkenes. With the loss of the *Orion* off the coast of Finnmark in December 1903, BDS ordered a new ship from the Bergens Mek shipyard. Ready in January 1905, she was named *Lyra,* with her machinery and boilers having been recycled from the condemned *Orion*, it enabled the construction costs to be kept down to 310,000 kroner.

Her accommodation differed in that instead of the first class dining room being farthest aft it was now located amidships on the main deck, just ahead of the boiler room. This gave greater comfort and would eventually become the common practice for future new builds. She continued to be a three-class ship with 42 first class berths aft, 20 second class berths midships (which were marketed as first class in the tourist season) and 42 forward in third class.

With both the *Lyra* and *Astraea* in service BDS now had two modern purpose-built vessels serving the Coastal Express route. In 1907, BDS and NFDS were awarded the contract for a fourth weekly round trip, with two services extended from Bergen to Vadsø and subsequently to Kirkenes as from 1st October 1908. The NFDS vessel, *Sigurd Jarl* (1884) was no stranger to the area having been transferred from its normal Hamburg – Vadso route and was comparatively fast at 12 knots. As from the autumn of 1907 the *Sigurd Jarl* took up the Bergen-Vadsø service under the command of Captain Axel Aarøe, the start of a long and distinguished 33-year career on the Coastal Express.

NEW BUILDS 1909 – 1912

Surprisingly, there had been few new purpose-built ships during the first two decades of Hurtigruten operation, the shipping companies preferring to cascade older vessels onto the route. The Coastal Express with its all year round service was still quite understandably viewed as a high-risk operation. It was not for another decade, after suffering war losses between 1914 and 1918, that ship owners actually started to insure their vessels. Older ships were obviously more expendable than younger ones. However, between 1909 and 1912 no less than four new and impressive looking ships would join the service.

The awarding of the contract to BDS and NFDS for the fourth

weekly round trip in 1907 had not gone down well with VDS who had proposed to transfer their *Andenaes* (1903) from other duties but it was rejected. In the event VDS decided to order a new ship to join the *Vesteraalen.* Built at the Trondhjems Mek shipyard the ship was named *Richard With,* after the founder of VDS, on 24th June 1909. For the first year the *Richard With* was under the command of Captain Frederik Hegge. At 905 gross tons she was the largest ship yet to be built for the route. The ship, designed for rough weather, had beautifully sharp lines complemented by a slightly sloping funnel which gave an impression of great speed. The design also called for both holds to be situated forward, which again meant that when fully laden she would bury her bow rather deep in the water and as a consequence affect manoeuvrability. As new, the hull was painted white but as from 1914 became black, in line with other vessels on the Coastal Express.

The *Richard With* was to have a long career before being torpedoed and sunk off Rolvsøya, north of Hammerfest with much loss of life in September 1941.

The opening of the Bergen to Christiania (Oslo) railway in 1909 offered new opportunities for the city of Bergen. BDS capitalised on the event to order a new and larger ship to further strengthen their grip on Bergen as a hub for both the Coastal Express and their North Searoutes. A product of the local Bergens Mek Shipyard, she was expensive to build at 504,000 kroner entering service in June 1910 as the *Midnatsol* (978 gross tons). She had an elegant profile with fine lines to the bow and stern and was the first coastal steamer to have the bridge placed above all the other decks which, with the dining room immediately below on the shelter deck, gave the ship a rather majesterial look.

Her long career saw her safely negotiate two world wars, but in 1949, with a new *Midnatsol* being constructed at Ancona, Italy her name was changed to *Sylvia.* She finished service on 10th October 1950 and was immediately towed away for scrapping by SA Elba of Antwerp.

Following the loss of the *Astræa* off Florø in January 1910, BDS immediately commissioned her replacement from the Burmeister and Wain Shipyard in Copenhagen, being delivered as the *Polarlys* in April 1912. Having her named in Christiania, the Norwegian capital, was an advertising masterstroke as it brought together all the various parliamentary, local government and transport authorities.

The *Polarlys* (1,069 gross tons) looked superb in her BDS black and white livery and was some six feet longer than her consort at 208 feet. There were cabins for 141 passengers spread over three classes. Part of the hold was insulated and was fitted with cooling systems.

This ship too was to have an extremely long career, remaining coal fired to the end of her service finishing her last voyage on 11th October 1951. With an overdue passenger certificate she was laid

In 1910 BDS introduced their new flagship *Midnatsol*, seen dressed overall for the occasion. *(Mittet)*

up in Bergen, and in deference to a new *Polarlys* taking shape on the stocks at Aarhus, she too was temporarily renamed *Sylvia.*

A new career awaited as the Royal Norwegian Navy bought her to act as a 'mother ship' to their motor torpedo boat (MTB) fleet as KNM *Valkyrie.* She was to serve the Navy for another ten years before being finally scrapped in 1963.

VDS had, not surprisingly, felt rather marginalised as to the way the Coastal Express was developing, for having been the initiators to make the route possible, the next three new contracts had all gone to their competitors. However, the contract awarded in 1911 for a weekly fifth service did go to VDS for a sailing between Bergen and Vadsø, initially to be covered by the *Richard With*, while the older *Vesteraalen* took over the Trondheim-Tromsø sailings. It was only intended to be a temporary deployment, as in August 1911 VDS ordered a new and larger vessel from Trondhjems Mek. The *Finmarken,* as she was named (note the spelling), entered service on 7th September 1912 and was to serve the route for 44 years, only being scrapped in 1960 just two years short of her 50th birthday.

Capable of making 14.5 knots, she was the largest and fastest ship on the route (1,119 gross tons) and building on previous experience, an extra hold had been created aft of the engine room. The interior decoration was of the highest order, the passenger accommodation keeping to the traditional layout of first class amidships and aft, second class forward of this with third class towards the bow. There was also a first class dining room for 70 people as well as a smoking and music lounge at the stern.

The *Finmarken* was to become a legend in her time, a greyhound with a sleek white painted hull and large funnel complemented by the VDS blue boot topping. Captain Hegge transferred his command to her, later to be succeeded by Captain Ragnar Falck. Her entry into service marked the end of any more new builds on the Coastal Express for another 13 years until the *Dronning Maud* was delivered in 1925 for NFDS.

Captain Fredrik Ottar Hegge and the *Finmarken* were by all

Two years later in 1912 BDS introduced their Danish built *Polarlys* captured here arriving at Sandnessjøen. *(Mittet)*

accounts inseparable right up to his retirement in 1929. He earned the reputation of being able to find his way around even in the most difficult weather conditions. A well known tale records the time when in thick fog approaching Svolvær in the Lofotens, he asked the lookout if he could see anything. 'No', was the reply. 'Put your hand out, can you feel anything?' 'Yes, wood' was the reply. They were safely berthed.

The ship continued in service until 1956, when with a new *Finnmarken* (note the new spelling) on the stocks at Blohm and Voss, Hamburg, her name was changed to *Vågan*. The ship was sold to Sjøguttskole Rogaland, Stavanger and renamed *Gann* for use as a youth training ship. Withdrawn in late 1960 she was sold for scrapping in the Netherlands. However, before she left Norway her first class smokeroom was dismantled and presented to Bergens

Nearly forty years later a BDS postcard from 1950 of the *Polarlys* at Finsnes; today spelt as Finnsnes. *(Bård Kolltviet Collection)*

Summer cruises to the Land of the Midnight Sun and Svalbard have always been a major tourism attraction.

The 'graceful greyhound' *Finmarken* (1912) is viewed approaching Molde. *(Bård Kolltviet Collection)*

Sjøfartsmuseum. Most of her interior was sold to a local Dutch entrepreneur who intended to reuse some of it in a new motel, but in the end it was resold to become part of 'Villa Finmarken' in Beekbergen, near Apeldoorn. In 2003 some of these furnishings and rooms were returned to Norway and now form part of the exhibition

at the Hurtigruten Museum in Stokmarknes. The *Finmarken* of 1912 still lives on!

TO THE LAND OF THE MIDNIGHT SUN – Part 1 to 1914

The seeds for today's tourist industry along Norway's 'long coast'

The *Finmarken*'s crew in serious pose for the camera. *(Hurtigrutemuseet)*

A royal occasion (possibly at Trondheim) for the *Finmarken.*
(Hurtigrutemuseet)

Elegance personified: NFDS' *Sigurd Jarl* (1894) is beautifully observed by
Anders Beer Wilse early on in her long career. *((Norwegian Maritime Museum)*

began to germinate in the middle part of the 19th century when regular steamship sailings between Britain and Norway were started. Once accessibility had been established some of the more intrepid visitors began to use the Government mail steamer services to venture further afield.

It was not, however, until the 1870s that tourism to the north began to gain any momentum. The Coronation of King Oscar II at the Nidaros Cathedral in Trondheim on 18th July 1873 and the monarch's subsequent travels along the coast to Nordkapp, changed perceptions completely, especially as the journey was followed by a host of journalists from all over Europe reporting back their

experiences. Paul du Chaillu, a Frenchman, who made visits to northern Norway in 1871 and 1878, published his experiences in a two-volume book entitled 'The Land of the Midnight Sun'. This title caught the public's imagination and is still used profusely today. The publication also aroused the interest of Thomas Cook & Sons, the London travel agency, which in 1875 organised the first ever escorted excursion to Nordkapp.

Both BDS and NFDS would use their newest ships with their higher standards of accommodation to exploit this new business opportunity. From 1878, steamers on their Hamburg to Vadsø service were diverted round the northern side of Magerøy during the

NFDS' fine looking *Kong Harald* (1890) is seen at the Festningskaien, Bergen. *(Bjørn Andersen Collection)*

Another image of **Kong Harald,** this time with a white hull viewed in Trondheimsfjord. *(Anders Beer Wilse)*

VDS' **Andenæs** spent much of her career sporting a white hull for her summer cruises to the Land of the Midnight Sun. *(Anders Beer Wilse/Mittet)*

summer months so that passengers could visit Nordkapp, being put ashore either at Gjesvær or Kjelvik before taking the path up the 300 metre high cliffs.

In 1883, BDS and NFDS decided to offer their own series of weekly cruises from Trondheim to Nordkapp expanding to twice weekly in 1884. By 1889 the cruise programme had expanded so much that four ships were needed for the cruises and publicity became more elaborate, evolving from simple newspaper advertisements in 1883 to a 72 page, full colour, multi-lingual brochure by the early 1900s.

Cruising also created new demands on the ships' masters as in addition to having to command the ship, they also had to be able to speak several foreign languages. Not only that, they were also responsible for arranging the shore excursions and on-board entertainment!

VDS did not get into the act until 1907 when they began cruises to Nordkapp from Trondheim, using their *Andenæs* (1903). For her popular cruising rôle in the summer she was given a white hull. These cruises continued until 1913, with the *Andenæs* sailing from Trondheim to Narvik and then on to Tromsø and Nordkapp where a stay of several hours gave passengers ample time to ascend to the high plateau. On the southbound run, visits were made to Trollfjorden and Torghatten (near Brønnøysund).

SVALBARD ADVENTURES to 1914

Around 400 nautical miles to the northwest of Nordkapp is the Svalbard archipelago, of which Spitsbergen is the largest island. For four months in the winter there is no sunlight and the islands are in the grip of the Arctic pack ice. From late April, however, the ice retreats sometimes beyond the 80°N mark. On shore, rare and colourful Arctic flowers blossom and temperatures can become quite comfortable.

Whilst the Dutch had exploited the natural resources of Svalbard

during the late sixteenth and early seventeenth centuries, by 1645 the archipelago was left to the explorers, scientists, mineral prospectors and wandering polar bears until the late 1800s.

BDS's *Pallas* was the first steamer to make a cruise to Svalbard in 1881, chartered by Henry Clodius of Tromsø with about 60 people making bookings. The voyage was plagued by drift ice and bad weather, which meant that the time spent on Svalbard was shorter than planned. Complaints later appeared in several newspapers with the excursion being dubbed (possibly unfairly) as 'The Spitsbergen Swindle'.

Fridtjhof Nansen's explorations on board the *Fram* between 1893 and 1896 attracted worldwide interest in the polar region. The more adventurous tourists wanted to follow in his footsteps, at least for part of the way.

It was Richard With (who else!) who took up the challenge, proposing a series of weekly cruises from Hammerfest to Adventfjorden, on the west coast. In mid June 1896, Captain With took the 1873-built *Raftsund* (689 gross tons) north to Adventfjorden with a team of builders and a cargo of timber. They arrived there on 17th June, precisely 300 years to the day since the archipelago had been discovered by William Barents. The building materials were used for the construction of a small hotel, which featured a balcony, a heated lounge, and beds for up to 30 guests.

Using the *Lofoten*, and promoted as 'The Sportsman's Route', the VDS Svalbard cruise itinerary involved a departure from Hammerfest at midnight every Tuesday (connecting with the Coastal Express) and an arrival at Adventfjorden on the Friday morning. The return trip via Nordkapp started the same evening, with Hammerfest being reached late on Monday morning. Eight cruises were offered seasonally in the years 1896 to 1898 with around 60 passengers carried annually. However, with increasing competition from larger cruise liners, coupled with finding it difficult to make a profit, VDS decided to pull out.

The *Hera* (1899) did not come onto the Coastal Express until 1913, here she is at Vadsø. *(Bård Kolltviet collection)*

The hotel was closed but remained on the company's books until it was sold to John M. Longyear, who had acquired coal mining concessions on the shores of Adventfjorden in 1904. The building was converted into the mining company's office, and the small town of Longyearbyen grew up around it. Although seemingly abandoning their cruising activities, VDS continued to use the *Lofoten* on lucrative private charters to the area until 1910 before re-launching a Svalbard cruise programme using the *Andenæs,* this time with Trondheim as the departure point. Not to be outdone, BDS and NFDS followed suit with their *Erling Jarl* and *Kong Harald,* their cruises starting from as far afield as Hamburg and Antwerp.

GROWTH 1913 – 1914 and …..

Between 1892 and 1914 there was a steady expansion of services, both in frequency and length as passengers and forwarders of perishable goods transferred their allegiances from the slower 'kombinerte' services. However, operating results were prone to fluctuation, as were profit levels between the three companies and between the individual steamers. In both 1903 and 1905, VDS, with only the one steamer, recorded profits of 60,000 kroner on their Hurtigruten sailings. Early records indicate that their passenger numbers had shown a rapid increase from just over 6 000 in 1893 to over 70 000 in 1916.

The steady expansion of services also came with increasing costs in both fuel and labour and as a result profit margins became tighter. Additionally, whilst some new and faster vessels had come onto the route, the number of intermediate ports of call had increased (Beian,

Indre Kvarøy and Finnsnes had been added to the timetable) so that the service from Trondheim now took longer than it did in 1894, with schedules being based on the speed of the slowest vessels on the route. In addition, the larger a ship's cargo capacity then the longer it took to handle it.

In 1913 BDS introduced the *Hera* (1899) as a running mate for their *Midnatsol* and *Polarlys* replacing the rather slow *Lyra,* originally designed as a combined cargo and passenger ship for services between Hull and Scandinavia. Whilst she had a certificate for 600 passengers, her cabin accommodation was for only 58 in three classes, but she did have a useful service speed of 12 knots of speed and a large refrigerated hold for fresh fish, ideal for the Coastal Express. With the introduction of five sailings per week from Bergen to Kirkenes as from 1st July 1914, it now meant that ten ships were needed to run the service and as a result NFDS were forced to turn to their veteran *Haakon Jarl* (1874) for the route. Originally constructed for the Hamburg–Finnmark service, she had long ago in 1887 played host to Prins Gustav and Princesse Victoria on their voyage to the Nordkapp. The ship was lavishly furnished including adjustable cabin heating.

…. RETRENCHMENT - WORLD WAR ONE

Even though not directly involved in the First World War, Norwegian commerce fearing that the North Sea would become a battleground and effectively blockade the country, experienced panic buying and a rush on the banks. When the realisation came that the war was going to be centred on Belgium and Northern France, some

The *Haakon Jarl* (1874) was already 40 years old when introduced onto the Coastal Express in 1914. Pictured near Tromsø in the 1880's. *(Axel Lindahl)*

Formerly DSD's flagship, the *Kong Haakon* (1904), nearest the camera, is seemingly dwarfed by other ships at Bergen in 1925. *(Anders Beer Wilse)*

degree of normality returned, albeit with few tourists. As the priority had to be for cargo during 1915/16, the *Capella* was converted into a freighter, saloons and staterooms gave space for hatches and cargo, the ship returning to serve on the long freight route between Oslo and Finnmark. As a precaution ships had neutrality markings painted on their hull sides, illuminated at night. On the down side coal supplies were becoming very scarce as in 1915 Britain had placed an embargo on foreign exports. Schedules were slowed down in order to save coal consumption. It was welcome news in 1916 that the Arctic Coal Company (USA) based at Longyearbyen (Svalbard) had been persuaded to sell off their coal mines to a Norwegian consortium which included some of the coastal steamer operators.

On the Coastal Express itself, 1917 saw the service reduced to only three sailings a week between Bergen and Hammerfest together with two from Trondheim to Kirkenes.

POST WAR BLUES 1918 – 1923

The end of the First World War saw the Coastal Express enhanced as from July 1919 with a sixth weekly round trip. The upshot was that older tonnage had to be drafted on to the service in order to fulfil the requirements. NFDS's *Olaf Trygvesøn* (1876), named after the King of Norway from 995 to 1000 was one of the steamers to be drafted in as a temporary replacement on the Coastal Express, though was later to be seen more regularly on the route between 1919 and 1921.

With this expansion came a new company to the route, Det Stavangerske Dampskibsselskab (DSD). Over the following six decades the company's three red rings around the black funnel would become a familiar sight along the coastline. Indeed this company is still very much in evidence today along the Norwegian coastline with interests in sea freight services through Nor Lines AS

and in transport and tourism through Norled AS. DSD's involvement meant a further extension of the route to Stavanger and although this ceased in 1936, the company remained as part of the Hurtigruten organisation until 1979.

The *Kong Haakon* (1904) became the first DSD ship to serve on the Coastal Express remaining there until 1927 when the ship returned to its original Oslo – Bergen route run jointly with Det Arendals Dampskibsselskab. The ship's long career included a return to the Coastal Express in 1942, which entailed a change of name to *Kong Sverre* by order of Quisling's Nasjonal Samling (National Government). With no less than 13 vessels now required to maintain six weekly departures on the route, it was fortunate for NFDS that the restructuring of activities on their Hamburg route meant that they now had ships to spare, one of which was the 29-year old *Kong Harald* (1890). Indeed, the ship had been on the Coastal Express route in a relief capacity since the spring of 1919 and had gained the reputation of being a sturdy and comfortable ship. The *Kong Harald* was only retired in 1950 after running aground near Florø, finally being scrapped at Bruges in 1954 at the age of 64 years.

The *Kong Harald* was joined by her near sister ship *Neptun* (1890) from BDS. However, this post war boom was not to last long and effectively came to an end in 1920. Inflation was rife as Norway along with the rest of Europe suffered an economic recession. Output was down, unemployment was up and there was industrial unrest. For the Coastal Express companies, in May 1921 a number of their vessels had to be laid up when stokers, seamen and engineers walked out on strike. It was to be six weeks before they returned. The *Neptun's* brief Hurtigruten service came to an end in October 1921 when the Coastal Express was reduced by one weekly round trip and the ship returned to her original Hamburg service, later to be scrapped in 1926. Compared to her sister, it was a very

The elderly *Neptun* (1890) was another ship with a forward cargo hold issue, at speed her bow could dip disconcertingly. *(Anders Beer Wilse/Norwegian Maritime Museum)*

NFDS' elegant *Haakon VII* photographed by Anders Beer Wilse when new in 1907. *(Bjørn Andersen Collection)*

short career indeed.

The recession had also caused NFDS to withdraw their *Haakon VII* (1,347 gross tons) from the Trondheim – Bergen – Newcastle service. When delivered from Trondheim Mek in 1907, the vessel was Norway's largest ever passenger ship. With staterooms for 144 passengers, this three class ship set a new trend in design with the lounges stretching across the full width of the main deck. In a bold move, the *Haakon VII* was reactivated and placed in service on the Coastal Express for the summer of 1922. The ship became an immediate success and a much sought after ship on which to travel.

NFDS' *Olaf Trygvesøn* (1876) would see Hurtigruten service only late in her career between 1916 and 1921. *(Jørgen Wikstrøm/ Trondheim Byarchiv)*

CHAPTER THREE

Expansion

RISØYRENNA

Until 1922 all Coastal Express services had called at Svolvær (Lofotens) before sailing to the east of Hinnøya via Lødingen and on to Harstad, marginalising the prosperous area of Vesteraalen where Richard With, founder of Hurtigruten had his headquarters. At Risøyhamn, where he lived, was a narrow shallow channel separating the islands of Hinnøya and Andøya. As a Member of the Storting (Parliament) from 1910 he had begun to petition the Norwegian Government to have this channel dredged so that it could take larger steamers. After protracted debate the finance was found and in July 1911 the work commenced to excavate the hard stony bed of the channel but by 1913 it was increasingly evident that the dredger wasn't up to the job. They had to wait an interminable time until the spring of 1920 before a new dredger, Ekskavator 6, had been built and was able to restart work. It was finally completed and ready for opening in 1922 at a cost of around 3 million kroner.

The new channel was 5km (3 miles) long, 50m (160 feet) wide with a minimum depth of 5m (15 feet). It was a magnificent achievement and one of national pride and importance. VDS's

Finmarken was appropriately chosen to carry King Haakon, Norwegian President Jahren, Richard With and other dignitaries from Trondheim to Risøyhamn. At 23.00 on 24th June 1922, leading a flotilla of more than 400 craft, the *Finmarken*, with Captain Hegge, Richard With, pilot Anders Holte and the official party on the bridge, steamed through the Risøyrenna channel, her bow bursting through the 80m long banners at either end amid a cacophony of ships sirens and

VDS' *Finmarken* at the opening ceremony of the Risøyrenna Channel in 1922. *(Hurtigrutemuseet)*

whistles, the 'star turn' being the *Ekskavator 6* which, as a way of welcoming the distinguished guests, noisily set all her machinery into motion.

From 1st July 1922, two of the five weekly coastal express services were diverted after Svolvær to travel through the Raftsundet onto Stokmarknes, Sortland, Risøyhamn and Harstad. This gradually increased in frequency and today the Risøyrenna channel is now the norm for all Hurtigruten vessels. As compensation for the change a 'replacement' route from Narvik, via Lødingen to Svolvær was put in place. This route, connecting Ofoten with Lofoten, lasted for 80 years until it ceased in January 2003.

In 1957, further dredging work was required to deepen and widen the channel which took until 1966 to finally complete. Later, in September 1997, with new and larger ships now in service, further deepening of the Risøyrenna was undertaken lasting until September 2001 when the *Narvik* (1982) officially reopened the channel. The need to further deepen this channel is very evident as the 'millennium' class Hurtigruten ships are said to have only 200 mm (8 inches!) under their keel when the tide is at its lowest. After the *Trollfjord* touched the bottom in 2011, further dredging took place in 2013, with the spoil being used in development of the Norwegian Coastal Authority's 'Pure Project' at Harstad.

CONSOLIDATION 1924 – 1939

In 1924, in order to give better continuity, a new six year contract was agreed, though with a reduction in service levels with only three sailings per week to Kirkenes from Bergen, one from Stavanger and one from Trondheim. However, journey times from Kirkenes to Trondheim were reduced by no fewer than eight hours. Previously in 1921, Trondheim had strengthened its importance as an interchange between rail and steamer services when the new direct railway line from Oslo (Dovrebanen) was opened, further reducing journey times between the two cities.

In thick fog on the night of 17th June 1924 some six nautical miles off the island of Landegøde, just north of Bodø, the *Haakon Jarl* collided with the southbound ship, *Kong Harald*, sinking in eight short minutes with the loss of 17 lives. Both captains were acquitted of any blame at the subsequent inquest, blame being laid solely on the poor visibility prevailing at the time. The tragedy shook the nation, a reminder of the constant challenge between nature's capricious whims and human vigilance.

The loss of the *Haakon Jarl* saw the *Haakon VII* on the route permanently as from 1924 and in keeping with changing needs, the ship was converted into a two class vessel as from 1926.

The situation prompted NFDS to order the first new ship on the Coastal Express service since the *Finmarken* in 1912. The vessel was said to be a 'radically improved' version of BDS's *Midnatsol* and *Polarlys,* which was not surprising as they were now 15 years old. Built by the Fredrikstad Mek Shipyard, the *Dronning Maud* (1,505 gross tons) was formally handed over on 3rd July 1925. With a non 'in house' interior designer being employed for the first time the ship had a totally different feel; first class was now amidships with large

A 1930's image of the NFDS vessels *Dronning Maud* and *Prinsesse Ragnhild* at Ålesund. *(Bård Kolltviet Collection)*

DSD's *Sanct Svithun* photographed early in her career, possibly prior to her inaugural voyage in 1927.

lounges and each cabin had running hot and cold water. Reputed to have cost just over 1 million kroner it was expensive, but money well spent. Indeed, according to a popular tale, after the celebratory inaugural lunch held on board at Trondheim, a number of the NFDS directors and guests went aft to the 3rd class lounge, thinking that they were in the 1st class accommodation! The machinery was of the traditional triple expansion type and her boilers were still coal-fired, reflecting that it was still the cheapest and most readily available fuel, especially as they were now able to source it from Svalbard. On trials the ship achieved 16.25 knots, though her service speed was to be around 13 knots.

Det Stavangerske Dampskibsselskab (DSD) followed suit in 1926 ordering its first ever purpose built ship to serve on the route from the International Shipbuilding & Engineering Co. Ltd, Danzig (Gdansk). Named *Sanct Svithun* in honour of Stavanger Cathedral's patron saint, the ship was ready for service on 30th June 1927. Designed as a two-class ship, she had 82 first class berths

amidships with 100 third class berths forward. The ship had a full promenade deck, a substantial boat deck, above which was the chartroom and wheelhouse. Still coal fired, the *Sanct Svithun* was built at a cost of just over 1 million kroner, considerably cheaper than any of the more local Norwegian shipyards could quote, and would prove to be a particularly good sea boat.

In 1927 with business recovering, the service again expanded to six weekly round trips, with five from Bergen and one from Stavanger. As with previous expansions, a number of older ships were again cascaded onto the route, BDS choosing their 37-year old *Mira* (1891), which was hardly a move forward. VDS used their newish small local steamer *Mosken* (1924) over the next five years albeit mostly in a relief capacity. For NFDS it was to be the *Kong Gudrød* (1910) which in 1929 replaced the withdrawn *Haakon Adalstein*, even though the ship was not entirely suited to the Coastal Express.

The *Haakon VII's* new career was to be rather short lived, as

NFDS' *Dronning Maud* on the occasion of her maiden voyage July 1925. *(Ole Skarbø)*

A powerful 1930's Mittet postcard portrait of BDS' *Mira*. *(Author's Collection)*

around 22.30 on 6th October 1929, with heavy rain and gale force winds, the ship deviated from the normal course just south of Florø, hit rocks, rolled over onto her starboard side, and sank by the stern. Nine passengers and nine crew members were lost, many of them trapped in the stern section. The *Haakon VII's* Boatswain, Anders Andersen, in an act of heroism, managed to transfer 55 people from the bow onto land, where they found shelter. They were rescued three hours later by the Spanish vessel, *Elin Jens San Lucar* and brought safely to Florø.

The ship remained where she lay all winter until March 1930 when she was patched up and towed to the Laksevåg dry dock, Bergen. The damage was so great that the *Haakon VII* was sent to Stavanger for scrapping. BDS also used their *Mercur* (1883) as a relief vessel on the Coastal Express throughout the 1930s. She was something of a survivor having had a number of almost obligatory groundings, including a sinking in her early days.

Following the success of the *Sanct Svithun* being built as a two-class ship, others followed with both *the Midnatsol* and *Polarlys* having significant refurbishments in 1930 after which they appeared with berths for 35 first class passengers and for 46 in third class.

On the night of 17th/18th March 1931, the *Hera* was southbound from Honningsvåg to Hammerfest, battling against a head wind in heavy seas and adverse currents, when she grounded on an unlit headland near Havøysund. The sea was too rough for the *Hera's* crew to attempt to launch the lifeboats so the second officer, Einar Ramm, tied a rope around his waist, leaped overboard and swam ashore. A form of breeches buoy was rigged up, using two lifebelts tied together and whilst six people were swept away and drowned, a

A BDS image of their elderly *Irma* (1905) at full speed, often nicknamed the 'submarine.' *(Bjørn Andersen Collection)*

total of 56 managed to scramble to safety. Einar Ramm subsequently received a medal for his bravery.

BDS had already earmarked *Irma* (1905) to replace *Hera* when the tragic loss of the company's oldest vessel occurred. *Irma's* stately interiors were designed with international travel in mind, with smart lounges and berths for up to 140 passengers in different configurations depending on the season. She was normally was seen on the Nordkapp and Spitsbergen cruises until 1931, when she was scheduled to take over from the ill-fated *Hera*. In reality, she wasn't a particularly good sea-boat as she tended to dip into the waves earning her the nickname of 'the submarine'.

Following the loss of the *Haakon VII* in 1929, NFDS immediately ordered a replacement ship from the Fredrikstad Mek Shipyard at a

A rare image of the BDS steamer *Mercur* (1883) which survived a number of mishaps in her career *(Fred Hawks/ Bård Kolltviet Collection)*

The elegant lines of NFDS' 1931 new build *Prinsesse Ragnhild* off Bodø are seen to full effect in this Mittet postcard. *(Bjørn Andersen Collection)*

cost of 1.47 million kroner. Named *Prinsesse Ragnhild* (after the daughter of Crown Prins Olav) she was introduced onto the Coastal Express on the 25th November 1931.

She had a more modern feel about her, not just in the layout, but also in her technical equipment, with sonar and an electronic log installed as standard. The shipyard's technical director, K G Meldahl had designed a 'steam motor', a double compound engine capable of developing 2,500 ihp, giving a speed of 16.5 knots, not dissimilar to the Lenz compound engine fitted to the *Sanct Svithun,* but much more powerful. Less modern, her boilers remained coal-fired, although they were more fuel-efficient.

For VDS a replacement for the *Vesteraalen*, now 38 years old, was now becoming a matter of some urgency. A long running industrial dispute at the Fredrikstad Mek Shipyard delayed completion of the new 1.3 million kroner *Lofoten* (1,571 gross tons) until February 1932. For the first time all cabins had running hot and

cold water. Refrigerated cargo holds for the carriage of fresh fish were sited both fore and aft. VDS preferred a more conventional 2,200 ihp FMV triple-expansion engine as propulsion, which enabled the ship to achieve 17.25 knots during trials. Under the command of Captain Alf Korneliussen, the *Lofoten's* first departure from the Fortress Quay at Bergen was on 24th February 1932.

With her boilers being converted to oil firing in 1948, it was not until 1964 (now renamed *Vågan*) that the *Lofoten* was finally retired. Her new life as a cruise ship in the Mediterranean was to be short, being broken up in Haifa only two years later after a serious onboard fire.

THE BLUE RIBAND OF VESTFJORD

The area between Svolvær (Lofotens) and Bodø (Nordland) is known as the Vestfjord and involves a 70-mile sea passage. Traditionally, whenever a new vessel took up service on the Coastal

Not to be outdone VDS introduced their new *Lofoten* in 1932, seen here off Trondheim. *(Schrøder /Author's Collection)*

There's plenty of interesting social history in this rare colour post war image of the **Lofoten** at Trondheim. *(Bjørn Andersen Collection)*

Express, the crossing of this open stretch of water gave ships' masters the chance to show just what their new charge could do and any passage time close to four hours was considered be to excellent. Gradually the *Dronning Maud*, *Haakon VII* and *Finmarken* reduced it, until in 1930, the *Prinsesse Ragnhild* broke the 'four hour barrier' with a time of 3 hours 56 minutes. In 1932, the *Lofoten* further lowered this to 3 hours 51 minutes only for the *Prinsesse Ragnhild* to regain the unofficial 'Blue Riband' with a time of 3 hours 41 minutes. This feat put any further attempts to lower the mark well out of reach until the spring of 1950 when NFDS's new motorship, *Erling Jarl,* cut another six minutes off the time bringing it down to 3 hours 35 minutes. Today, ships sail via Stamsund from Svolvær to Bodø

and vice versa, lengthening the journey time.

'THE NORDLAND TARIFF BATTLE'

During the inter-war years, as the economy gradually recovered, the Coastal Express route between Trondheim, Bodø and Harstad became a battleground between various competing companies. This stretch of the coastline is by far the most profitable in terms of the amount of freight it generates. With roads almost impassable in winter and no direct railway between Trondheim, Narvik and Bodø the coastal steamers represented the best means of communication between the ports. A number of local companies vied for trade along this coastline and saw the Coastal Express as a rival to their

Ofoten's (ODS) **Nordnorge** as originally built, departing Trondheim in 1925. *(Author's Collection)*

This Schrøder image off Trondheim shows the newly lengthened and rebuilt **Nordnorge** taking up Coastal Express service in 1936. *(STFM)*

The *Stella Polaris* of 1927 was BDS' answer to the international cruise liners, seen here in Trollfjord in 1928. *(Author's Collection)*

wellbeing. Matters came to ahead with a price war breaking out as Det Ofotens Dampskibsselskab (ODS), Det Saltens Dampskibsselskab (SDS) and Det Helgelandske Dampskibsselskab (HDS), who jointly ran the services along the Nordland area of the west coast, took on the Coastal Express undercutting them through use of the subsidies they were getting for their local services. The express companies cried 'foul' as they were contracted not just to serve these areas but also the less profitable regions of Troms and Finnmark and felt that trade should be on an equal footing with rivals not able to 'cherry pick' only the lucrative elements. BDS, NFDS and VDS had all been forced to slash their freight rates by up to 50% as well introduce new, competing and unprofitable services. Nobody benefited, and the dispute rumbled on until all parties came together in August 1935 to thrash out an agreement under which local operators could not start up new routes in direct competition with those provided by the Coastal Express. With the Norwegian Government also proposing that a daily departure be introduced, ODS then offered their flagship, *Nordnorge*, to the service. As part of the deal a weekly call at Narvik, an important transport, commercial and industrial centre, was introduced.

The *Nordnorge* (991 gross tons) was of classic proportions, dating from 1924 having been built at Trondhjems Mek, designed specifically for the ODS Narvik to Trondheim service. When it became clear in 1936 that the ship would be engaged on the Coastal Express service she was again sent to Trondheim for rebuilding into a two-class ship and lengthened. Refrigerated compartments were fitted in her holds, an observation lounge was built at the forward end of her promenade deck, the bridge and chartroom being moved one deck higher. New navigational aids were installed including an echo sounder, electric log and radio telephone. Whilst externally she was a very imposing vessel, some felt that internally she had lost some of her former elegance. The *Nordnorge* proved to be ideally suited to the Coastal Express and what she lacked in speed was offset by her handling capabilities which enabled her to get alongside quays very quickly.

SHIP TO SHORE COMMUNICATION

During the 1920s communications to and from ships on the Coastal Express were, in the main, reliant on telephone calls from one port to another. Although by 1927 the Norwegian Government had set up a network of coastal radio stations along the whole of the coastline a degree of complacency still reigned and whilst it was not unusual for Coastal Express ships to be delayed in poor weather, nobody actually knew where they were, creating anxiety for those waiting for their arrival.

However, it was the *Polarlys* incident on 13th February 1930 which really jolted the conscience of the Coastal Express companies. The ship was en route to Trondheim and having departed Rørvik was crossing the Folla (Folda) in deteriorating weather conditions. The *Polarlys* had been passed by the northbound *Finmarken,* when at around 23.00 a freak wave smashed in the starboard door to the first class foyer, flooding several cabins. By midnight it was becoming increasing difficult to steer the ship in almost nil visibility. Both Captain Norlie and his pilot, Alfred Petersen, became increasingly uncertain as to their position. They decided to steam west in order to ride out the storm. The *Polarlys* was due to arrive at Trondheim at 06.00 the next morning, but by the afternoon with no sign of her, the local newspaper, *Arbeider-Avisen*, was carrying the headline '*Polarlys* lost on Folla overnight?' Early in the evening, the weather began to abate enough for the *Polarlys* to attempt to claw her way towards Trondheim. She was spotted passing the Agdenes lighthouse at the end of Trondheimsfjorden around 23.00, finally arriving at Trondheim in the early hours of the next morning (15th). The Captain and crew were feted as heroes but the incident wasn't forgotten.

Pressure from the Norwegian Seamen's Union, businessmen and the media took up the cause so effectively that by the end of the year the *Dronning Maud* was fitted with a radio telephone. It was first used on 3rd January 1931 when a call was made by *Arbeider-Avisen* to the ship as she crossed the Folla en route to Rørvik. It was an unqualified success and by 1936 all Coastal Express steamers had been equipped with radio telephones.

TO THE LAND OF THE MIDNIGHT SUN – Part 2 to 1939

In the years immediately after the Great War, large foreign registered cruise liners began to dominate the Nordkapp cruise scene bringing in both European and North American visitors, who generally chose to travel on ships registered at European ports, since the USA's prohibition laws ensured that their own vessels were 'dry'.

As far as the Coastal Express companies were concerned, with six round trips scheduled each week, they were now finding it difficult to release ships suitable for the summer cruises from Bergen to Nordkapp. New strategies would be needed.

BDS restarted their cruises in 1921 using the former HAPAG cruise liner *Meteor*. On account of the prohibitive Norwegian laws concerning the sale of alcohol, for the first year she sailed under the Red Ensign. This venture became so successful that in 1925 BDS ordered a larger and even more luxurious cruise liner, the *Stella Polaris* (5,208 gross tons), at that time the largest vessel to have been built in a Scandinavian shipyard. In spite of her size, the diesel powered ship had cabin accommodation for just 200 passengers. In June 1927 the *Stella Polaris* made the first of a series of summer

cruises to Nordkapp and Svalbard, setting a pattern which continued through to 1939.

With the *Irma* and *Haakon VII* no longer needed on their North Sea services, NFDS too restarted their popular 14-day cruises from Bergen to Nordkapp in the summer of 1922. Additionally, the *Irma* undertook a three-week cruise to Svalbard. Neither ship, however, was ideal for the up market clientele their owners were keen to attract to Norway.

The solution for NFDS was to purchase the Royal Yacht *Alexandra* (1,728 gross tons) in 1925. Launched in Glasgow in 1907, she was intended to be King Edward VII's private yacht as well as for informal use by the Royal Family. A graceful ship, she boasted three masts, a clipper bow complete with bowsprit and two imposing bell topped funnels. Powered by three Parsons turbines, she had a voracious appetite for coal. Renamed *Prins Olav*, her first Nordkapp cruise commenced from Bergen on the 5th July 1925.

The recession, which set in during the early 1930s, coupled with increasing competition from foreign 'floating hotels' and her own high operating costs, all conspired together to hammer nails into the *Prins Olav*'s coffin as far as cruising was concerned. In 1936/1937 the former Royal Yacht underwent another major facelift, this time for a new career as a Coastal Express ship. The transformation had to be seen to be believed.

VDS however, were not to return to cruising until 1927 when they introduced their local steamer *Mosken* (1924; 410 gross tons) on weekly departures from Narvik to Nordkapp. That same year, the three Coastal Express companies, in partnership with the Finnmark Tourist Board and the travel agencies of Thomas Bennett, Thomas Cook and Berg-Hansen, created Nordkapps Vel to promote tourism in that area. A landing stage, together with a pavilion and post office was built at Hornvika, adjacent to Nordkapp, at the base of the 300 metre high cliffs together with a new pathway up to the plateau.

By the end of the 1932 season, the *Mosken*'s cruises were no longer financially remunerative. However, the publicity for these trips

NFDS' *Tordenskjold* operated economy 'ilgodsruten' cruises to Nordkapp each summer in the 1930's; photographed off Svolvær by Anders Beer Wilse. *(Galleri NOR)*

In addition to Coastal Express relief sailings VDS used their *Mosken* on weekly summer cruises from Narvik to Nordkapp between 1927 and 1932. *(Norwegian Maritime Museum)*

TFDS' *Lyngen* in Isfjorden, Longyearbyen, on one of her summer visits to Svalbard. *(Harald Grindal)*

had not been wasted as it had generated a considerable number of additional bookings by foreign tourists for the Hurtigruten steamers.

Other initiatives included using NFDS's *Tordenskjold*, whose Trondheim to Hammerfest freight service was extended in the summer months to Honningsvåg for Nordkapp. This became very popular with freelance tourists as a cheap cruise, known as the 'ilgodsruten'.

It was the Coastal Express, in the difficult economic climate of the 1930s, which provided the answer to how best to cater for those growing numbers of tourists who wanted to see Norway close up

rather from the remoteness of the decks of a 'floating hotel'. Together with the major travel agencies, they petitioned the Storting's Tourism Committee for permission to advertise package holiday round trips on the service.

Significantly, they also requested that in summer vessels could sail north of Magerøy and call at Hornvika to enable passengers to visit Nordkapp. By 1934, with permission granted, the Coastal Express began to attract passengers in even greater numbers from all over the world. Colourful brochures were produced to publicise the 'new' service and even canvas swimming pools were erected on the promenade decks if space permitted!

SVALBARD ADVENTURES 1918 - 1939

It was not until 1933 that the Storting finally agreed to financially support a regular passenger and mail service to Svalbard during the summer months, for which Troms Fylkes Dampskibsselskap (TFDS) would receive an annual subsidy of 20,000 kroner using their largest and newest steamer, *Lyngen* (489 gross tons), built in 1931 by Trondhjems Mek.

Starting from Tromsø, calls were made at Bjørnøya, Longyearbyen and Ny-Ålesund to deliver supplies and mail. Of the five round trips made in 1934, 181 passengers were carried, of whom 51 were round-trip tourists, 45 travelling to or from Svalbard on business and 85 using the steamer between intermediate ports.

In 1935, 285 passengers were carried, while freight traffic was boosted following the opening of a new fishing base at Ny-Ålesund.

NFDS' *Prins Olav* (ex *Royal Yacht Alexandra*) totally transformed seen here arriving at Svolvær on her 'maiden' voyage in 1937. *(Kristian Kanstad/Bjørn Andersen Collection)*

A BDS postcard of their 1937 built *Nordstjernen* at speed, looking very much a 'pocket liner'. *(Author's Collection)*

Each round trip lasted fourteen days. The outbreak of war would put an end to regular Svalbard sailings for another next twelve years.

A DAILY COASTAL EXPRESS

The new six-year contract, which came into being in 1936, required no fewer than fourteen steamers to run it. Each week there were to be five departures from Bergen to Kirkenes and one each from Stavanger and Trondheim to Kirkenes, the latter service including a call at Narvik, using the *Nordnorge*. This new proposal wasn't greeted with universal acclaim, particularly from those based in Troms and Finnmark, singling out the shortened Trondheim service for criticism. They argued that if this were extended to Bergen and the longer Stavanger service truncated at Bergen, you could have a much more balanced service, as well as eliminating the unpopular transfer of cargo, passengers and mail at Trondheim. Stavanger could be served by other means. This came into being in October 1936 and forms the basis of the service we see today.

During the negotiations for a daily service, both BDS and NFDS had committed themselves to the ordering of new tonnage for the route. However, NFDS then took the decision that rather than building a new ship, it would be more cost effective to rebuild their cruise steamer, the *Prins Olav*.

More than a few eyebrows were raised at the announcement as many felt that the money would be better spent on a new ship rather than a costly rejuvenation of one that was now approaching 30 years old. The *Prins Olav*'s emergence in the spring of 1937 from this 1.25 million kroner rebuild at Trondheim revealed that the ship had been totally transformed. The profile had been totally changed with the superstructure radically altered, the former clipper bow replaced by a raked 'soft nose' bow and the previous two bell topped funnels replaced by one large modern version. The *Prins Olav* now measured 2,147 gross tons, her length increased to 284.3 feet, whilst 'down below' the original turbine machinery had been replaced by a massive 3,500 ihp FMV double compound engine giving her a service speed of 17 knots. Two cargo holds, one forward and one aft had been created giving a refrigerated capacity for 5,000 cases of fresh fish. The accommodation was to a very high standard with the ship now configured as a two-class vessel certificated for 450 passengers.

Unlike NFDS, BDS opted for new tonnage, signing in 1936 a 1.9 million kroner contract with the Fredrikstad Mek Shipyard for its construction. It was to be the company's first new build for the Coastal Express since 1912. The delivery of the *Nordstjernen* (1,919 gross tons) was delayed by a couple of months owing to a small fire on board whilst being fitted out and so it was not until 15th June 1937 that she was formally handed over. With a passenger certificate for 590, most of the first class accommodation was to be found on the shelter deck with single and two berth cabins for 63 occupants, whilst third class had room for 92 in two and four berth cabins. All cabins were fitted with wash basins with hot and cold running water and the ventilation was provided by the new 'Thermotank' forced air system.

The crew accommodation was substantially improved with comfortable two and three berth cabins. Their working conditions

A rare image of BDS' *Ariadne* at Molde; she transferred to the Hurtigruten in December 1939 and would be sunk by enemy action just a year later.

career was to last a mere six months, as we shall see. VDS had previously ordered a new ship intended for their local Lofoten and Vesterålen services. Delivered in October 1940, the *Hadsel* (406 gross tons) was a motorship, with a very smart modern streamlined profile. Notwithstanding her propulsion unit, (a 6-cylinder MAN of 540 bhp, service speed 12 knots), it was her high degree of manoeuvrability that her Ka-Me-Wa variable pitch propellers afforded which caught the eye. It was a major advance and well ahead of her contemporaries on coastal services.

In April 1941 the *Hadsel* was chartered from VDS in April 1941, and was to become closely associated with the Coastal Express throughout the next decade before finally bowing out at Bergen on 31st March 1950, to be replaced by a new *Vesteraalen*. On 29th January 1958, in bad weather, the *Hadsel* struck rocks off Nakkmean, near Reine, Lofotens, tearing the bottom out of her engine room. Everyone, 20 passengers and 26 crew members managed to get away safely in the lifeboats. The ship then slid off the rocks and sank within three minutes.

In the meantime the high and heady days of 1930s idealism had ended abruptly in the stark reality of 1st September 1939 when Germany invaded Poland. The next six years would markedly affect the route and no less than 14 ships on the Coastal Express were to be lost.

were also enhanced as the ship had electric winches for cargo handling. An indicator of the changing needs of travellers was the provision of space for the carriage of cars, On Monday 21st June 1937, under the command of Captain Michael Kobrø, she made her first sailing.

A further two ships were to serve on the Coastal Express in 1939/1940 when the daily service to Kirkenes from Bergen finally became a reality on 5th December 1939. BDS introduced their 1930-built *Ariadne* (2,028 gross tons) to the route but her new

A Schrøder postcard view of VDS' *Hadsel* off Trondheim in 1941. *(Author's collection)*

CHAPTER FOUR

Invasion and Occupation

1939

In early October the Coastal Express services were reduced by two per week, leaving the *Midnatsol, Richard With, Kong Harald and Sigurd Jarl* laid up. Howls of protest, particularly from businesses based in Northern Norway, left the Ministry of Trade in no doubt as to the unpopularity of their decision and of the effects it would have, particularly on the fishing industry. By the end of October both the *Midnatsol* and *Kong Harald* were back in service, followed by the *Sigurd Jarl* a month later and the *Richard With* in mid December. The *Dronning Maud* and *Polarlys* spent several weeks making round trips from Trondheim to Tromsø. The *Polarlys* was then requisitioned by the Government and temporarily laid up at Bergen pending conversion into a hospital ship. As a result BDS introduced their *Ariadne* (1930) on the 4th December 1939 to help cover the six weekly round trip service now in force.

BDS' *Nova* was drafted in as an extra ship on the Coastal Express for the winter of 1939/40, but in June 1940 was ordered to escape to Britain to join the Notraship (Norwegian Shipping and Trade Mission) fleet. Prior to this, the *Nova* was normally to be found on the BDS Bergen to Torshavn and Reykjavik service.

1940

Norway's neutrality ended on 9th April when the country was invaded by Germany and the King and Parliament were forced to flee. Bergen was under siege, with three Coastal Express steamers (*Polarlys, Mira* and *Lofoten*) trapped at the port. The *Mira* became an accommodation vessel, *Polarlys* likewise, having the added ignominy of being renamed *Satan*, thankfully quickly shortened to *Tan* before reverting back to her original name by the end of the year. The first Coastal Express casualty of the war was the *Sigurd Jarl*, which was attacked by German planes and sank in shallow water near Molde, thankfully without loss of life. It was not until November 1942 that the ship was raised. NFDS considered putting her back in service but

NFDS' elegant **Dronning Maud** at the beginning of her career; she was the first hurtigrute ship to be lost in WW2, May 1940. *(Anders Beer Wilse)*

Although displaying Red Cross markings the **Dronning Maud** was attacked by German aircraft off Føldvik, Gratangen on 1st May 1940, catching fire before sinking.

the ship was beyond economic repair.

Only eight days later, on 1st May 1940, as the *Dronning Maud* approached the berth at Føldvik, Gratangen (Troms) and despite clearly displaying Red Cross signals and flags she was attacked by three German aircraft. Two bombs hit the forward hold and another crashed in between the bridge and funnel. The *Dronning Maud* immediately caught fire with 18 people being killed and 31 wounded in the attack. The burning wreck was towed away from the wooden pier before finally running aground and rolling over.

Despite stiff opposition, the German army gradually gained ground so that by May the southern terminus for the Coastal Express

This Schrøder postcard captures perfectly the graceful profile of VDS' **Finmarken** off Trondheim; she tried twice to escape to Britain in May and June 1940. *(Author's Collection)*

was now at Bodø. The *Finmarken,* under the command of Captain Falck, made an audacious attempt under the cover of fog on the night of 7th May to escape to the Shetlands with just a crew of seven, but her fuel reserves were too low and she only got as far as Stokmarknes.

Worse was to come on 10th May, when Det Ofotens Dampskibsselskab's *Nordnorge* was lost. She had been requisitioned and her crew replaced with German naval personnel. The previous day she had sailed from Trondheim with troops for Hemnesberget, close to Mo i Rana. She had been noted off Rørvik and this news was quickly passed on to the British Military Command. As she disembarked her troops she came under fire and with the Germans not wanting the ship to fall into the hands of the Allies, the sea cocks were opened and grenades thrown into her bilges, leaving her to sink. Two British destroyers (HMS *Carlisle* and HMS *Zulu*) then appeared and after almost simultaneous explosions, the *Nordnorge* drifted away from the quayside and sank in deep water.

By 6th June it was clear that Norway would have to capitulate. For this eventuality, Ole Siem, Shipping Director for Free Norway (and also Chairman of VDS) had prepared a plan to send to Scotland all steamers not essential for the maintenance of the Coastal Express. Each ship would need to take on coal and provisions for at least ten days' sailing.

Overnight on 7th/8th June, various ships slipped out of their hiding places and steamed westwards to Britain. Among them was

The powerful lines of NFDS' *Prins Olav* which was sunk in June 1940 whilst attempting in tandem with BDS' Ariadne to reach Britain. *(Bjørn Andersen Collection)*

the *Finmarken*, but around 100 miles from the Norwegian coast she was spotted by a German bomber which managed to score a hit on one of her lifeboats. Such was the force of the explosion that it sprang a leak in her hull. Making water, she was forced to turn back.

The loss of three ships in 17 days had already been acutely felt, but on 9th June 1940, less than a month later, came a double tragedy.

Both the *Prins Olav* and *Ariadne* were to have very short careers on the service, as whilst not new ships, they had not come onto the Coastal Express until 1937 and 1939 respectively. The *Prins Olav* had been requisitioned in May 1940 by the Norwegian military to assist in the evacuation of Helgeland and later to convey troops from Kirkenes to Gratangen (north of Tromsø). The ship received fresh

orders on 7th June 1940 to sail to Britain and headed to Hammerfest for bunkering. Likewise, the *Ariadne,* previously requisitioned to serve as a hospital ship and marked as such according to international rules. On 8th June with 54 people on board she headed west from Tromsø to try to reach Britain. The next day the two ships joined up and set course for Torshavn in the Faroe Islands. Around 22.30 that evening and 80 miles west of the Lofotens, both ships suffered a sustained attack from six enemy bombers. Despite the fact that the *Ariadne* was protected by the Geneva Convention, she was the first to be attacked receiving direct hits on the bow and funnel casing and began to sink. Eight were killed in the attack but the crew and passengers were able to get into lifeboats. The *Prins Olav* with her superior speed tried to escape through repeated

A freezing Vadsø in early 1940 with BDS' *Ariadne* anchored in the harbour, clearly displaying her neutrality markings. *(Trygve Gjervan/Trondheim Archive)*

NFDS' *Prinsesse Ragnhild* was torpedoed just off Landegøde, near Bodø by the British submarine HMS *Taku* in October 1940. Over 400 persons lost their lives. *(Author's Collection)*

course changes but failed to do so. Given the ferocity of the attack, fatalities were fortunately very low with just one from the *Prins Olav*. Four lifeboats, two from each steamer, managed to link together. As the lifeboats from the *Prins Olav* were larger than *Ariadne's*, survivors were exchanged between them, to improve buoyancy and reduce crowding. Around 03.00 on 10th June, the lifeboats were spotted by British destroyer HMS *Arrow* and the survivors were taken to Scapa Flow. The same day the capitulation of Norway officially took place, when German troops entered Tromsø.

Coastal Express sailings did not properly resume until early July 1940. There was some optimism that the tonnage situation would soon be eased, as NFDS had managed to purchase the relatively modern Copenhagen to Rønne overnight ferry *Bornholm* to help fill the gap. However, it would be another two years before she was ready to enter service as *Ragnvald Jarl*. VDS had the luxury of a new build, the *Hadsel*, which was delivered in October 1940, but straightaway was chartered to NFDS as their needs were greatest. Det Nordlandske Dampskipsselskap (NDS) also purchased a ship from Sweden, *Hansa*, which became their *Skjerstad*, entering service in December 1940.

War losses again hit the Coastal Express on the 23rd October 1940, when the *Prinsesse Ragnhild* became the first steamer to be lost whilst on an ordinary service as, when northbound from Bodø,

just off Landegøde, a powerful explosion ripped open her keel. On board were least 400 passengers together with a crew of 50. Two small coasters in the vicinity rescued 156 persons, but over 300 perished. The precise cause was a mystery until many years later when it was revealed that her attacker was the British submarine HMS *Taku*.

1941

In January 1941, daily Coastal Express sailings between Trondheim and Hammerfest were resumed and whilst there were only two extended services to Bergen each week, Kirkenes fared better with a near daily service.

On the morning of 4th March 1941, *Mira*, en route to Harstad from Svolvær was intercepted by the British destroyer HMS *Bedouin* at the entrance to the Raftsundet. A warning shot was fired across her bows, but she continued at full speed. A second shot, fired into the forward part of her hull, failed to produce any response from those on her bridge. Inevitably the destroyer let fly a whole volley of shots, one of which struck the ship just below her funnel, rupturing vital pipework. Coming to a stop, she was then evacuated and once her lifeboats were clear the destroyer fired another salvo sending the *Mira* to the bottom. Seven people died as a result of this incident. The wounded were taken by HMS *Bedouin* to Aberdeen for hospital

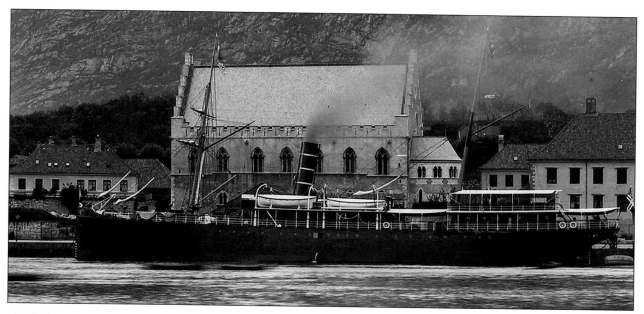

BDS' *Mira* seen early on in her career at Bergen. In March 1941 she was sunk by HMS Bedouin in the Raftsundet after failing to heave to.

treatment. It transpired later that a German officer had run up to the bridge and held the *Mira's* Captain at gunpoint to ensure that he did not obey the commands from the British destroyer.

Operating the Coastal Express in wartime was not easy, as many lighthouses, channel markers and lighted buoys had been deliberately put out of action. Sailings were restricted to daylight hours as was cargo handling so as not to contravene the blackout regulations. It was also deemed prudent that, when crossing open stretches of water, ships should do so in convoys, although this led to some vessels being used as 'shields' in case of attack from Allied aircraft.

On 30th August 1941 the *Midnatsol* was en route from Hammerfest to Tromsø and approaching Øksfjord. It was a fine, sunny afternoon and a German convoy had been observed approaching from the opposite direction. At 15.30 there was a violent explosion and one of the supply ships, the *Donau*, was enveloped in smoke. This was followed by a second explosion as the ship following her, the *Bahía Laura*, was also torpedoed and caught fire. The *Midnatsol*, barely half a mile away, stopped and lowered all four of her lifeboats, rescuing around 200 survivors, later unconfirmed reports suggested that between 1,000 and 2,000 others were killed or drowned. The attack was presumed to have come from a British or Russian submarine.

Two weeks later, 13th September 1941, was another day of

The 1912 built *Midnatsol*, in wartime markings, photographed approaching Brønnøysund in 1943. *(Nordland Museum)*

VDS' *Richard With* was torpedoed by HMS *Tigris* off Rolvsøy, north of Hammerfest in September 1941; she sank within 50 seconds, 65 passengers and 28 crew were drowned. *(VDS archive)*

double losses on the Coastal Express, though this time it was in separate incidents.

The first sinking on this day was off the Nordland coast. After the loss of the *Nordnorge* in 1940, Det Ofotens Dampskibsselskab had been using their smaller *Barøy* (1929) on the service from Trondheim to Narvik. At 03.50 on her way north towards Tranøy on the Nordland coast, the *Barøy* was hit on the port side by a torpedo from an aircraft operating from the carrier HMS *Victorious*. The ship sank almost immediately. Unconfirmed figures suggest that there were 68 Norwegian and 37 German passengers together with 26 crew members on board. It was fortunate that the *Skjerstad* was nearby and observing unusual flotsam in the dark managed to stop and pick up 19 survivors. Later that day a BBC broadcast from London stated that a 'large transport ship' had been bombed and sunk off Nordland. It would seem that the *Barøy* had been mistaken for another vessel which had been in the area a few hours before.

The second incident happened a few hours later, the *Richard With* was returning from Honningsvåg to Hammerfest. The ship had arrived there the previous day but was ordered not to proceed any further in the direction of Kirkenes because of high levels of submarine activity. Around 11.00 whilst passing Rolvsøy, the ship was rocked by an explosion and immediately began to sink stern first. Only able to launch one lifeboat, passengers and crew just had to grab anything buoyant they could find. Eye witness accounts say that she sank within 50 seconds. The fishing vessel *Skolpen* was close by and managed to pick up 32 survivors, but at least 65 passengers and 28 crew members lost their lives. The blame was put on a marauding Russian submarine, but years later it was

revealed the perpetrator was the British submarine HMS *Tigris*.

As a result, all services north of Hammerfest were suspended as the risk for large steamers was now too great and a substitute service, (the 'Erstatningshurtigruten') to Kirkenes would be set up using smaller vessels until such time that matters improved.

As a temporary measure Finnmarkens Fylkesrederi (FFR) offered to provide a service using the *Tanahorn* (built 1910) and *Alta* (ex *Alten*, built 1906). There was a subsequent change of plan with all normal Coastal Express sailings being terminated at Tromsø. From there to Skjervøy, Øksfjord and Hammerfest, the *Vesteraalen* was rostered to provide a fast connecting shuttle service; it was a high-risk decision as it involved crossing open waters.

Barely a month later, on 17th October 1941, the *Vesteraalen* went the same way as the *Richard With*. With 39 passengers on board, the ship had left Tromsø earlier that afternoon and was now closing in on Øksfjord. Around 15.30 there was a loud explosion and the ship broke in two, the bow sinking almost immediately and the rest of the ship doing so about thirty seconds later. There were only seven survivors, whilst 60 others lost their lives as nearly everyone was below decks at the time of the attack. It was later confirmed that the *Vesteraalen* had been torpedoed by the Russian submarine SHCH-402. There were, thankfully, to be no more Coastal Express losses for another 15 months.

1942

Under the occupying powers many sections of Norwegian society were subjected to harassment and persecution if they did not conform to doctrines and edicts. Among the decrees passed was one making it compulsory for teachers to join the Nazi-controlled Lærersamband (Teachers' Union). Out of Norway's 14,000 schoolteachers, some 12,000 declared in writing that they would have absolutely nothing to do with such an organisation. The inevitable upshot was the arrest of many of them.

On Sunday, 12th April 1942, 498 arrested teachers were brought on board the NDS vessel *Skjerstad* (passenger certificate 250) under armed guard. They sailed north for Kirkenes, where for part of the journey the *Skjerstad* acted as a shield for the German transport ship *Santos*. With numerous delays and after enduring inhuman conditions for nearly 17 days the prisoners were finally landed. Their reward would be heavy manual labour at one of the infamous Organisation Todt camps scattered around Festning (Fortress) Kirkenes. News of this spread rapidly throughout the country and the consequent tide of anger and wave of protests were so great that six months later the teachers were released and sent south.

There was a sequel to this story, when in the summer of 1950, many of the teachers returned to do the same journey in the same ship, this time as an act of pilgrimage.

Matters began to improve when in July 1942 a new NFDS ship *Sigurd Jarl* finally entered service over a year late owing to delays in obtaining materials. Originally ordered in 1939, as a cargo ship for their Bergen, London and Mediterranean Sea services, war losses had forced NFDS to have her completed as a vessel suitable for the Coastal Express.

Very much a converted freighter, the *Sigurd Jarl* was the largest Coastal Express ship to date (2,335 gross tons) and although rather slower than other vessels at 14 knots, the ship was ideal for the service at this period, when capacity was far more important than speed. The ship was only in service for four months before being requisitioned for use as a recreation ship for the occupying forces, not resuming on the Coastal Express service until 1944.

The *Sigurd Jarl* was useful to the route in that she had cavernous holds, albeit a sometimes double-edged benefit. On one occasion the ship spent a whole day loading fish at Svolvær, but when on arrival at Trondheim there was insufficient space in the transit sheds for such a cargo and she had to be diverted to Stavanger. This was fine when there was still a great deal of slack in the schedules but with new ships arriving on the scene, the sedate 13 or 14 knots service speed was becoming an issue. The *Sigurd Jarl* lasted until 1960 when she was sold as the *Xin Hua* to the People's Republic of China.

The other 'new' NFDS ship, the *Ragnvald Jarl* (ex *Bornholm*), finally entered service on 30th October 1942 after a refit lasting over two years again as a result of difficulties in obtaining materials. She too was comparatively slow, which in post war years was to become a major handicap. Formerly a Danish overnight motor ship owned by Bornholm Dampskipsaktieselskapet, Rønne, the *Bornholm* dated

A 1933 Mittet postcard of a furiously smoking *Vesteraalen*, she too was sunk in October 1941, this time by the Russian submarine SHCH-402.

from 1930 and had been built by Burmeister & Wain, Copenhagen. The ship, now named *Ragnvald Jarl*, reappeared as a compact, simple and modern addition to the Coastal Express, sailing between Trondheim and Tromsø. After nearly two years on the route, on 21st September 1944 the vessel was requisitioned by German authorities as a transport ship for the wounded during the evacuation of Finnmark.

Whilst the *Ragnald Jarl* had many good qualities, speed and manoeuvring ability were not amongst them. With new vessels being delivered from both Italy and Denmark in the period 1949 – 1952 and further new tonnage planned, the decision was taken to sell her as soon as practicable. Temporarily renamed *Harald Jarl* the ship was sold in July 1956 to Lübeck Linie GmbH, Germany as the *Nordland* for a cruising role around the Baltic Sea and Norwegian coastline. It wasn't until April 1974 that the ship was finally scrapped at Bilbao.

1943

For almost two years no further Coastal Express ships were lost through military action but on the last day of September came

The overnight Danish diesel ferry *Bornholm* is seen here at her home port of Rønne, she finally became NFDS' *Ragnvald Jarl* in 1942.
(Bornholm Museum)

61

Transformed in 1942 from *Bornholm* to *Ragnvald Jarl* the ship is pictured off Nordkapp in a NFDS publicity postcard. *(Bård Kolltviet Collection)*

DSD's *Sanct Svithun*, was lost as a result of enemy bomber action in September 1943 near Ervik, whilst southbound from Ålesund. *(Bjørn Andersen Collection)*

disaster. The *Sanct Svithun* departed southbound from Ålesund into a strong southwest wind and heavy sea, forcing the ship to reduce speed. At 18.45, six planes swept in low dropping bombs and strafing the decks with machine gunfire.

The *Sanct Svithun* was immediately ablaze amidships and so fierce was the heat that the lifeboat davits melted. However, with the engine still running and steering gear undamaged, Captain Alshager ordered the helmsman to steer for land, almost making it but fetching up on Kobbeholmen, a rocky islet, a couple of hundred metres from the shore, with her bows held fast. Olav Iversen, a deckhand, taking a lightweight hauling line which was attached to a ten-inch thick manila hawser, climbed down and was able drag and loop the manila hawser over a rock. This escape route was extremely difficult as the hawser would change from taut to slack in an instant. In all, 21 people crossed to safety by this means. Of the 121 people known to have been on board, 41 lost their lives, including 19 members of the crew.

The ship was beyond salvaging and some days later slid off the rocks and sank. The ship's bell, was salvaged and placed in nearby Ervik Church as a memorial to the events of that night. The inscription reads:

''To the people of Ervik
in appreciation of the rescue of human lives
when s/s *Sanct Svithun* went down
on 30th September 1943"

1944

On Sunday, 12th February 1944, after making her usual calls at Florø, Måløy and Ålesund, the BDS vessel *Irma* proceeded across the open Hustadvika at full speed. A tremendous explosion ripped the bows off the ship, her foremast crashing down across her bridge. A second explosion came from the vicinity of the engine room and the *Irma* heeled over to port, sinking fast. There was no time to launch the lifeboats but her six life rafts floated to the surface as she went down. The cargo ship *Henry* was nearby and managed to lower two lifeboats before she too was torpedoed and sunk. A total of 61 crew and passengers from the *Irma* were lost and only 25 survived.

At the subsequent inquiry, it was revealed that the *Irma* had been spotted by two Shetland based, Norwegian crewed, motor torpedo boats (MTB *653* and MTB *627*) with orders to sink any cargo shipping in that area. Why they failed to observe the neutrality markings is not understood. Thankfully this would the last loss the service would suffer during the conflict.

Two months later at 08.40 on 20th April 1944 Bergen was rocked by a massive explosion after a cargo of dynamite on board the Dutch ammunition ship *Voorbode* erupted, killing 23 people and injuring many more. Moored next to the *Voorbode* was the *Kong Sverre*, the name having been changed from *Kong Haakon* in 1942 on the orders of the Quisling Government. She was badly damaged and had to go to Stavanger for repairs, not returning to Coastal Express service until January 1946.

From 20th June 1944 there were to be five Hurtigruten sailings per week; two from Bergen and three from Trondheim, all terminating at Tromsø. The whole service had inevitably become less and less reliable as the fortunes of war changed in Finnmark. The *Nordstjernen*, already on trooping duties (her Norwegian crew paid off) was ordered on 20th September to Øst-Finnmark. The following day the *Ragnvald Jarl* was requisitioned, which was a mistake since there was a severe shortage of diesel fuel in Norway. The ship was laid up at once. A month later, the *Lofoten* was adapted into a floating field hospital, but allowed to retain her Norwegian crew.

FINAL DAYS 1945

The New Year of 1945 brought with it severe coal and oil shortages and one vessel after another had to be laid up. By March, the fuel crisis meant that the Coastal Express was only able to operate a single weekly departure in each direction using the only three ships still operational, the *Sigurd Jarl*, *Lofoten* and *Finmarken*.

On 7th May the occupying forces surrendered and the rightful Norwegian administrative and political organisations assumed responsibility for the day-to-day running of the country once again. Crown Prince Olav returned from London on 13th May, accompanied by most of the members of the exiled Norwegian Government. There were great celebrations when King Haakon returned to the capital on 7th June.

Already, the Coastal Express companies were making plans for revival and recovery once peace eventually returned to Europe.

ERSTATNINGSHURTIGRUTEN - The Compensation or Replacement Route

The loss of the *Richard With* in 1941 had highlighted just how dangerous it was for vessels to sail between Tromsø and Kirkenes and that an alternative means was needed. With the cooperation of the three main Coastal Express companies, (VDS, BDS and NFDS) the Ministry and German Military agreed to a 'replacement service' using smaller vessels, particularly those which had a reasonable hold capacity.

The Erstatningshurtigruten, to give it its official title, initially operated between Vadsø and Hammerfest (later extended to Tromsø). For the short crossing across the Varangerfjord to Kirkenes two larger vessels were retained as it was felt it would give some sense of normality and not arouse unwanted curiosity from the Russian batteries sited opposite on Fiskarhalvøya.

VDS had overall control of the operation, the *Skandfer*, at 36 gross tons, is recorded as the smallest and the *Grinnøy* at 135 gross tons, the largest. From just six vessels chartered in November 1941 this had increased to 27 vessels by May 1943. Fixed itineraries were established with six departures from Tromsø; two to Vadsø, two to Båtsfjord and two to Hammerfest each week. In addition the Post Office also chartered a number of small craft exclusively for the

BDS' *Irma* was sunk without explanation by two Shetland based, Norwegian crewed MTBs whilst crossing the Hustavika, south of Kristiansund, in February 1944. *(Bjørn Andersen Collection)*

The *Morild II* served right up to the end on the Erstatningshurtigruten; she was built in Hamburg in 1904 and was a mere 76 feet long and measured just 49grt. *(Terje Iversen)*

carriage of mail.

During its three years of operation, the Erstatningshurtigruten vessels carried more than 25,000 passengers, 181,673 mailbags northbound and a further 50,696 mailbags southbound. The *Grinnøy*, alone, is said to have made 55 trips between January 1942 and October 1944 mostly to Vardø, carrying 90,000 sacks of mail.

The 'prize' for the most valuable cargo probably went to the *Polarfjell*, captained by Hans Sorensen, when she carried over two million kroner in banknotes from the Norges Bank bound for Vadsø. One of the crew, Andreas Johnsen, concealed it under the mattress of his bunk, thinking it safer than being in with the mail bags.

It was a challenging route to operate on as they sailed in any weather along an open coastline without lights and beacons, having to run the gauntlet of marauding British or Russian submarines and avoid the ever dangerous floating mines. Whilst several vessels came under attack, miraculously only three were recorded as lost, the *Vaaland* in January 1942, the *Moder II* and *Uløya* in May and July 1944 respectively.

As they abandoned Finnmark in the autumn of 1944, the German troops employed a 'scorched earth' policy in order to hinder the Russians. Every settlement, every building and quayside was destroyed and lines of communication, roads and telegraph wires cut. It was also decided that the civilian population should be evacuated, not for its own safety, but so that no support or shelter would be on hand for the Russians as they advanced westwards.

The Erstatningshurtigruten now had to be abandoned as it was too dangerous to continue. The last sailing was, appropriately, by the *Skandfer* which reached Tromsø at 21.00 on Sunday 29th October. A few Erstatningshurtigruten boat owners organised their own evacuations; the owner of the *Morild II* on the morning of 14th November sailed into Kvalfjord, loaded all his furniture and belongings from his home onto the boat, and headed off south. Later that same day the building was burnt to the ground.

Fleet Renewal

POST WAR RELIEF

The shortage of post war tonnage brought once again a number of replacement ships to the Coastal Express. Perhaps the most significant event was the introduction in November 1945 of Det Nordlandske Dampskipsselskap (NDS) to the Hurtigruten consortium. The company dated from 1927 and operated out of Bodø in the Nordland region. With their original *Skjerstad* having been sunk in 1940, the company purchased the *Hansa*, a ship dating from 1925 which had been built for services to Lübeck from the west coast of Sweden. Renamed *Skjerstad* and mainly used on the Bodø – Trondheim service, the ship came through the war relatively unscathed though, when off the Nordland coast on the night of 13th/14th September 1941, she was able to rescue survivors from the *Barøy* after she had been sunk by a torpedo from a British aircraft operating from HMS *Victorious*.

In April 1943, NDS sent the *Skjerstad* for an extensive rebuild; not because it was an urgent priority but because sending her to a shipyard for a couple of years was less risky than keeping her in service. It was predicted, quite correctly, that once the war was over there would be a severe shortage of tonnage on the coastal services. Her rebuild at the Pusnes Mek Shipyard, Arendal, Southern Norway, was protracted and it was not until mid-May 1945 that the work really started in earnest. Once the Norwegian Ministry of Labour learned what was going on, NDS received a request that *Skjerstad* should be placed on the Coastal Express, as ODS were unable to provide suitable tonnage.

Her first few years as a Coastal Express steamer were quite eventful as on 3rd July 1946 she went aground near the lighthouse on Grinna Folla in fog. All 420 passengers were saved but repairs took three months. NDS used their elderly *Saltdal* (1884) as a temporary replacement.

In December 1947, the *Skjerstad* was sent to Trondhjems Mek to be converted to oil firing. Ready to resume service on 26th January 1948, she was berthed outside the entrance to the shipyard, where she was joined by the Fosen steamer *Yrjar*. The next morning revealed that the *Yrjar* had heeled over and dragged the *Skjerstad* with her. Both ships had sunk and were lying on their sides half submerged. Whilst it did not take long to raise them, the *Skjerstad* now needed an even more extensive refit, and was not ready to return until early July.

In the early 1950s NDS were informed that if they wished to remain in the consortium they would have to provide new tonnage as the *Skjerstad* was no longer considered suitable. A number of plans were drawn up but none came to fruition. In September 1958 the ship was withdrawn from service, to be replaced by the *Salten*.

The newest and most suitable ship to come onto the Coastal Express was the diminutive *Lyngen* (489 gross tons) built in 1931 for Troms Fylkes Dampskibsselskap for their longer routes around Northern Norway and very much the TFDS 'flagship'. At the end of hostilities between August and November 1945, the *Lyngen* was drafted on to the service. In 1947, she was placed on the Tromsø – Kirkenes link, which was timetabled to dovetail with the previous Monday's service from Bergen. From February 1948, the ship was

Seen here off Trondheim, NDS' ***Skjerstad***, which after her post war rebuild saw service on the Coastal Express from 1945. *(STFM)*

TFDS' diminutive ***Lyngen*** (1931) at Tromsø was also drafted on to the Coastal Express after the war; she was the last coal fired steamer to serve on the route. *(Arthur Sjøten)*

BDS' *Lyra* (1912) was rather slow at 11 knots used mainly in a relief capacity on the Coastal Express between 1945 and 1953. *(National Library)*

The *Ottar Jarl* was an unusual choice by NFDS to serve on the Coastal Express as a temporary replacement for the *Sigurd Jarl* in 1947/8. She was designed as a reefer ship albeit with passenger accommodation. *(STFM)*

chartered by VDS for thirteen months as a replacement for their *Lofoten* which was under repair.

Very much associated with Svalbard, in 1934 the *Lyngen* had started a regular passenger, mail and cargo summer service from Tromsø (later extended to Narvik) to Longyearbyen and Ny-Ålesund. Backed by an annual subsidy from the Norwegian Parliament, the route was widely used both by people who worked around Svalbard as well as tourists. These voyages were resumed in the summer of 1951 and continued until her final season in 1965 when, as the route's last coal-fired steamer, she was laid up in Tromsø.

The *Lyngen* was sold in January 1966 and renamed *Alfred Jensen,* after her new owner, being rebuilt into a diesel powered cargo/fishing boat. She remained active until 1984 but was finally condemned and scuttled off Harstad on 2nd July 1987.

Another vessel hastily brought into service was BDS' *Lyra* dating from 1912. Her Achilles heel was a lack of speed, a mere 11 knots. In the First World War, she had been captured by the Russian Navy to be used as a troop transport before being converted to minelayer in 1915. Sold to BDS for service between Bergen, Torshavn and Reykjavik, she escaped to Britain to become part of the Nortraship fleet (Norwegian Shipping and Trade Mission). She returned to Norway in the spring of 1945 to serve mainly on the BDS Bergen to Newcastle route but also in a relief capacity on the Coastal Express between 1945 and 1953. In February 1954 she was sold for use on pilgrim services linking Lebanon, Egypt and Jeddah (for Mecca). On 9th July 1958 she ran aground off Tor in the Red Sea and sank.

Two other short-term charters of interest were two 1929 builds, the *Ottar Jarl* and the *Oslo.* The former was quite unlike anything else seen before on the route and had been built as a diesel engined cargo-passenger ship for service between Seattle and Alaska. In today's language she would have been known as a reefer, albeit with some passenger accommodation. Originally named the *W B Foshay,* she was requisitioned by US Army in 1941 and registered as *PR.803*

Northland. Surplus to army requirements, NFDS purchased the ship in 1946, renamed her *Ottar Jarl,* subsequently standing in on the Coastal Express from December 1947 until late February 1948, whilst the *Sigurd Jarl* was under repair.

The more conventional *Oslo* was chartered by NFDS in 1948 from Det Arendal Dampskibsselskab as a temporary six month replacement on the route for their *Kong Harald* which had gone for a major refit, before returning to her normal Oslo – Bergen route in June 1948.

The *Kong Harald* was to have a long career, only being finally retired in 1950 after running aground near Florø. She was finally scrapped at Bruges in 1954 at the age of 64 years.

TOWARDS STANDARDISATION 1949 – 1960

The big issue that had dogged the Coastal Express companies since its inception was the lack of standardisation. Ships on the route possessed an incredible range of ages, speeds, dimensions and capacities making the whole service quite inefficient as schedules had to match the performance of the slowest ship. Even the 'newest' ships such as the *Sigurd Jarl,* a converted freighter, and *Ragnvald Jarl* (*ex Bornholm*) had issues. For example, whilst the *Ragnald Jarl* had many good qualities, speed and manoeuvring ability were not amongst them. With new vessels being delivered from both Italy and Denmark in the period 1949 – 1952 and further new tonnage planned, the decision was taken to sell her as soon as practicable.

On 14th June 1945, all the four main companies agreed to work together on a standardisation project with BDS having the responsibility for plan preparation. Over the next few months their technical office churned out many variants, all of which would have one engine driving a single screw. They would be one class ships on which the cost of travel would be according to grade of cabin. Public rooms, lounges, a self-service cafeteria and a restaurant would all be

In August 1950 NFDS' *Sigurd Jarl* ran aground off Bygnes near Sortland, Vesterålen. *(Lofotposten)*

NDFS' *Erling Jarl* was the first of the 'Italia-Batene' ships to be built, she is seen here in a near state of completion at Ancona in 1949. *(Author's Collection)*

located amidships on the promenade deck.

In April 1946 the technical department turned out a final proposal; to have an overall length of 264 feet; a beam of 40 feet; the superstructure to be one continuous unit, extending almost to the stern, with all cargo space situated forward, maximising the area of the passenger accommodation. This became known as Project 94.

Of the thirteen shipyards from which estimates for the new ships were requested, the choice was whittled down to two, Aalborg Verft of Aalborg, Denmark, and Cantieri Navale Riuniti dell'Adriatico of Ancona, Italy, the latter being awarded the contract on 27th September 1946 as they had not only submitted the cheapest bid (six million kroner per ship) but had also promised delivery in 1948. Four ships, one per company, were to be ordered although neither BDS nor NFDS were happy with this arrangement as their greater war losses meant that they needed more than one ship. A new agreement was reached and a second ship each for BDS and NFDS would instead be built at Aalborg Verft, Denmark. Soon after, BDS ordered a further ship from the same Danish shipyard.

THE ITALIA-BÅTENE

The first of the four identical 'Italia-Båtene' to be completed at the Cantieri Riuniti dell'Adriatico Shipyard, Ancona was the *Erling Jarl* for NFDS. She was handed over on 15th August 1949, sailing for Norway the following day with the company's directors and guests on board. The maiden voyage from Bergen on 5th September 1949 marked a significant milestone for the Coastal Express as from now on all new builds would be motorships.

In terms of outward appearance, the *Erling Jarl* incorporated elements from BDS's earlier proposals. A two-class ship, she measured 2,098 gross tons and 268 feet in length. The ship had

A rare colour photograph of NFDS' *Ragnvald Jarl* approaching her berth at Bergen. *(Bruce Peter)*

An aerial view from 1965 of BDS' *Midnatsol* sailing southbound from Sortland. *(Widerøes Flyveselskap)*

Soaking up the sun on the cosy aft deck of the *Midnatsol* *(Hurtigrutemuseet)*

berths for 77 first and 108 second class passengers with a certificate for 575 when on the Coastal Express. Accommodation for both passengers and crew was of a high standard, whilst the navigational equipment reflected the massive technological advances made during (and on account of) the war, i.e. gyro-compass, radar, direction-finder, echo-sounder and electric log. The prime mover was an 8-cylinder 2,500 bhp Fiat diesel, driving a four bladed Ka-Me-Wa variable pitch propeller and giving a service speed of 16.5 knots. The great advantage of such propellers is that the angle of pitch can be adjusted to control both speed and movement ahead and astern, without the need to vary engine revolutions or direction, saving a great deal of wear and tear when executing complicated manoeuvres such as approaching and leaving quays. Movements could be controlled directly either from the bridge or from the engine room. The *Erling Jarl* cost 9.5 million kroner, a significant increase over the original estimate reflecting the substantial devaluation that the Norwegian currency had suffered since the end of the war.

On her first trip, under the command of Captain Paul Holm, the *Erling Jarl* broke the record for the fastest crossing between Bodø and Svolvær, lowering it to 3 hours and 35 minutes, so claiming the unofficial 'Vestfjord Blue Riband'.

On 8th January 1958, whilst the ship was docked at Bodø, fire broke out aft in the second class accommodation. Thick acrid smoke and heavy fumes filled the corridors and cabins and 14 people lost their lives. Although the damage to the ship was relatively light, the subsequent enquiry ordered that the main deck accommodation be refurbished using improved fire resistant materials. At the same time new emergency exits were to be provided. Subsequently, similar precautions were later put in place taken on her three Italian consorts.

Such was the pace of change over the next decade and a half that by 1964 the *Erling Jarl* had become the oldest ship on the Coastal Express at the age of 15 years.

The *Erling Jarl* celebrated her 30th birthday on 11th August 1979 and sailing that day from Bergen, dressed overall, was greeted by large crowds at each port of call along the coast. However, the ship's career was to be cut short less than a year later as on the 13th March 1980, en route from Bergen to Florø, she ran aground in the Steinsundet, near Solund. Although sustaining a considerable amount of damage to one side of the hull, the ship managed to return to Bergen for dry docking, but following an inspection, was declared a constructive total loss.

Reluctant to sell the ship immediately, NFDS had the *Erling Jarl* patched up and moored in Trondheim as a hotel ship during the summer of 1980. On 23rd October 1981 the ship was sold to Oslo Carriers of Høvik, renamed *Balder Earl,* for use as a hotel ship. Nothing came of this venture and the ship was laid up in Grimstad, near Bergen, before finally being scrapped by Belgian ship breakers in January 1985.

Barely three months after the *Erling Jarl,* the second 'Italia-Båtene' ship, BDS' new *Midnatsol,* was ready. Externally, in her black and white funnel colours, she could easily be mistaken for a more solid version of their 1937-built *Nordstjernen.* Her entry into service was more than timely for BDS as the previous *Midnatsol* (now renamed *Sylvia*), was almost 40 years old.

On 3rd December 1949, under the command of Captain Njål Kolbenstvedt, the *Midnatsol* departed from the Festningskaien (Fortress Quay), Bergen on her maiden Hurtigruten voyage. It was reported that as she left the berth the Ka-Me-Wa variable pitch propeller was still in the 'going astern' position and the *Midnatsol* had to drop both anchors very quickly in order to avoid ramming the quay behind her!

The new motor ships immediately proved to be considerably cheaper to operate than the ageing steamers as figures show that for 1950 the total fuel bill for the coal fired *Polarlys* (1912) came to 666,000 kroner whilst the new *Midnatsol's* diesel fuel cost 411,000 kroner, a saving of over 37%. The *Midnatsol* and her three sister

VDS' **Vesterålen** arriving at Svolvær on her maiden voyage, April 1950. *(Bjørn Andersen Collection)*

vessels were to gain a reputation for being notorious 'rollers' and many a journey could become rather too lively for passenger comfort.

By the time she retired on 2nd January 1983 (now renamed the *Midnatsol II*) she had been in service for thirty three years and made 900 round trips, travelling over 2.25 million nautical miles between Bergen and Kirkenes.

Purchased for use as a hotel ship, as the *Midnatsol Norge,* she found use under successive owners but whilst being refitted at the Sarpsborg Mek Shipyard, Greåker, near Olso, on 8th February 1987, water poured in through an open valve, causing the ship to capsize.

Condemned for scrapping, the ship was towed away to Belgium two months later in May 1987.

The third of the quartet of vessels ordered from Cantieri Riuniti dell'Adriatico was the *Vesterålen* (note the spelling) which was delivered on 27th March 1950 and was the first 'new build' for VDS since their *Lofoten* in 1931. Although generally identical to *Erling Jarl* and *Midnatsol,* her decor reflected VDS's own special character and atmosphere. As a result of the serious fire on board the *Erling Jarl* in 1958, the *Vesterålen* had a major renovation, its second-class lounge made full width and the second-class dining room turned into a cafeteria.

An evocative colour image dating from 1955 of the **Vesterålen** at Trondheim; note the tank engine on shunting duties. *(Trondheim Byarkiv)*

DSD's *Sanct Svithun* arriving at Ålesund in 1952 with BDS' Midnatsol already berthed. *(Hurtigrutemuseet)*

The *Vesterålen* was in service for over thirty years and so it is not surprising she was involved in a few incidents, the worst being off the Hornelen, south of Måløy on 16th November 1978 when she was badly holed. With her pumps unable to cope, it was decided to beach her. There was considerable damage to her hull and her engine had been forced upwards by the impact. After costly repairs at Bergen, including renewing all her electrical wiring, the ship returned to service two months later, though with her engine still out of alignment it might have seemed that her Hurtigruten days were numbered, but not for another four years.

In January 1983 with a new ship nearing completion at Harstad, the *Vesterålen* was renamed *Vesterålen II* and was, by then, the last of the 'Italia-Båtene' still in service.

Sold to Northern Shipping AS of Oslo, with her name shortened to *Rålen,* she was then purchased by Fekete & Co in April 1984, who renamed her *Annexet* for use as a hotel ship in Tønsberg. In 1986, now at Drammen, she became a reception centre for asylum seekers and refugees. Resold and moved to Sundsvall in 1990, as the *Nordstjernen af Sundsvall,* within a year she had been purchased by Etoile Marine, Cyprus, again for further use as a hotel ship. The tow to the Mediterranean only reached as far as Rotterdam and after lying there for four years, the old *Vesterålen* was sold for scrapping at Vigo.

DSD would be the last of the Coastal Express companies to receive one of the 'Italia-Båtene'. The *Sanct Svithun*, named after Stavanger's patron saint, was launched on 18th May 1950 and was in such a complete state that her first test run was only two hours later, immediately achieving the full specification speed of 17 knots!

Known as the 'ambassador ship', the *Sanct Svithun's* maiden voyage was from Bergen on 8th June 1950. Although identical in

layout to its three sisters the décor, detailing and atmosphere very much reflected her Stavanger roots, the red funnel rings and the DSD motif on the bow being quite distinctive.

The *Sanct Svithun* is unfortunately mainly remembered for the greatest tragedy ever to hit the Coastal Express in peacetime. The ship was northbound from Trondheim to Rørvik on Sunday 21st October 1962 with 40 passengers, 2 postal clerks and 47 crew members on board. The ship followed the normal shipping lanes out into the Folla (Folda), but after this something became amiss.

At 22.00, a distress signal was received at Rørvik to the effect that the *Sanct Svithun* was sinking. For reasons still not totally clear, the ship had gone off course and grounded on rocks at Nordøyan, in the Folla. The grounding had ripped open her bottom and the ship had begun to sink. With her position being incorrectly reported search operations as a result were concentrated in the wrong place. 48 people survived but 42 died that night.

Many questions were raised, how could such an accident happen, with modern navigational aids and under normal weather conditions? How could experienced people not notice that the ship was on the wrong course? Sadly, the only people who could answer the questions, the duty pilot, mate and helmsman, all perished in the incident.

THE AALBORG TRIO

BDS's urgent need for more than one ship to replace their war losses, meant that they turned to Aalborg Værft, Denmark, for their second and third ships.

The first of the Danish vessels to be completed was the *Nordlys*, which was handed over at Aalborg on 12th May 1951. Under Captain Njål Kolbenstvedt she sailed for Oslo with 150 guests on

Busy times at Bodø with the arrival of the **Sanct Svithun** in 1960.
(Johnson & Sotberg)

board where a reception was held for King Haakon, members of the Storting and journalists. She reached Bergen on the morning of 17th May, making her maiden Hurtigruten sailing three days later. 1951 was an important year for Norway's oldest shipping company, Det Bergen Dampskibsselskab, as it would celebrate its centenary on the 12th December.

The design of the *Nordlys* (2,162 gross tons) owed much to the 'Project 94' proposals of the late 1940s with a compact superstructure and all public saloons at promenade deck level. The *Nordlys* was another step forward in the development of coastal vessels as the distinction between first and second class was abolished, a restaurant and a cafeteria replacing the previous separate dining saloons. Cabins with one, two and four berths were provided for 186 passengers and for the first time the price you paid for your voyage reflected the accommodation you chose. A passenger certificate was granted for 450 persons on coastal

voyages. Costing 8.5 million kroner, the *Nordlys* was cheaper than her four predecessors.

The ship's power plant was a 2,950 bhp 8-cylinder Burmeister & Wain diesel, giving a service speed of 15 knots. As with the Italian built ships, the *Nordlys* had a variable pitch propeller. Aluminium was used for all structures above boat deck level and with the bridge deck only half a deck higher than the boat deck, it offered greater stability. Her two holds were situated forward and worked by electric cranes instead of the old mast and boom arrangement.

Overall, the *Nordlys* introduced a new, clean, functional design to the Coastal Express, with her low profile dominated by the large black funnel with the white BDS rings around it, giving this Aalborg creation a very modern feel. The ship quickly gained the reputation of being a good sea boat, in sharp contrast to the notorious rolling of the Ancona quartet which were difficult to manoeuvre in high side-winds.

Thirty two years later, with three new ships scheduled to come into service, the *Nordlys* was laid up as from 23rd February 1983. She found some use an accommodation vessel particularly in conjunction with the Alexander L. Kielland Oil Platform, but other potential projects came to nothing and the ship began show signs of external deterioration. During the winter of 1987-1988 the *Nordlys* was being refurbished as a conference centre/restaurant to be based in Oslo, when on 13th April, fire broke out. The ship was condemned and sold for scrapping at Bilbao, Spain, but whilst under tow on 31st May 1988, she grounded off Farsund, Southern Norway, before sinking about 100km northwest of Texel, Netherlands.

NFDS's *Håkon Jarl* was the second of the Aalborg ships and was ready on 15th February 1952, some nine months after the *Nordlys*. In external appearance, the *Håkon Jarl* differed slightly in having a

BDS' **Nordlys** departing Hammerfest in July 1975, southbound for Tromsø. *(Mike Bent)*

Nordlys' Chief Engineer monitoring the control board in the engine room. *(Hurtigrutemuseet)*

Conditions could be rather cramped in the *Håkon Jarl* 's aft saloon as shown in this 1963 image. *(Aage Storlokken)*

mast with derricks on the foredeck, rather than electric cranes, and also had a tripod mast on her wheelhouse. The bridge deck was a full deck higher than the boat deck, the extra space gained being used for officers' accommodation. Unlike the two BDS vessels in the series, the ship had two 8-cylinder Atlas diesels geared to a single propeller, developing 3,040 bhp and giving a service speed of 16 knots. Curiously, the two smaller diesel units took up less space than one larger unit. Overall, the *Håkon Jarl* had the same internal configuration as the *Nordlys,* a one class ship with berths for 189 passengers, though the décor reflected the NFDS distinctive image.

The *Håkon Jarl* left Trondheim on her first Coastal Express sailing on 26th February 1952 with Captain Paul Holm as Master replacing FFR's (Finnmark Fylkesrederi og Rutelskap) *Alta*, which had been chartered by both NFDS and BDS as a 'stand in' until the new builds came into service.

With NFDS receiving permission in 1980 to build two new ships

replacing the *Erling Jarl* and *Håkon Jarl*, it came as a surprise when it became known that the *Håkon Jarl* would now be sold to Det Ofotens Dampskibsselskab (ODS) for NOK 8 million kroner and that ODS would now also take over one of the new builds. In January 1981, the *Håkon Jarl* was re-registered at Narvik and carried the Ofotens livery.

With the arrival of the new ODS ship *Narvik* on 18th December 1982, the *Håkon Jarl* was laid up at Narvik, with most of her crew being transferred to the *Nordnorge*. In order to prevent her on-board systems from malfunctioning in the cold weather, a crew of six had to stay on board, at a cost to the company of NOK 6,500 per day.

In January 1983, the ship was purchased by Fekete & Co. AS, Tønsberg, and renamed *Håkon Gamle,* shortly afterwards being resold to a consortium for use as a restaurant and hotel ship based at Pipervika, Oslo. At the same time her original name of *Håkon Jarl* was restored. The ship led a rather precarious existence after her

An excellent aerial view of NFDS' *Håkon Jarl* berthed at Sortland in June 1961. *(Vilhelm Skappel/ Widerøes Flyveselskap)*

From 1991 *Håkon Jarl* had a new career in Antwerp as a hotel and restaurant ship, seen here rather disfigured in 2004. *(Henk Jungerius)*

BDS' *Polarlys* arriving at Hammerfest from Havøysund in July 1975. *(Mike Bent)*

owners went bankrupt in 1988. In November 1991, she was towed to Antwerp, where, after renovation (and with its funnel back in NFDS colours), she opened in the following May as a hotel ship at the Bonaparte Dock, Antwerp, taking the name *Christian V*. Later in 1996, the ship was rather disfigured by the addition of a large structure aft of the funnel, remarketed as the *Diamond Princess,* her bow and stern still clearly stating *Håkon Jarl*. By March 2012, the ship's website was reporting that *'the Diamond Princess will be closed for reconstruction for an undetermined period'*. The following month she was removed from the Bonaparte Dock and moored upstream. On 11th August she was towed to Sluiskil, near Terneuzen (Netherlands) reportedly to be prepared for towing to Morocco. Nothing came of this and almost another 3 years passed before on 3rd June 2015 she was towed to Sloopbedrijf Gallo in Gent for scrapping.

The *Polarlys* was finally handed over by Aalborg Verft to BDS on 27th September 1952, some six months behind schedule. Her maiden voyage six days later marked the end of the first phase in the post war rejuvenation of the service as it was now possible to have daily departures north of Trondheim and five times a week from Bergen. Though excellent sea boats, the arrangement of two holds forward and machinery amidships meant that when fully laden the three Aalborg vessels were bow heavy and consequently more difficult to manoeuvre at speed.

In January 1979, together with the three other BDS ships (*Midnatsol, Nordlys* and *Nordstjernen*), the *Polarlys* was sold to Troms Fylkes Dampskibsselskap receiving the TFDS funnel livery and port of registry changed to Tromsø. After grounding near Sandnessjøen in November 1981, as part of the repair work at Bergen, a decision was taken to install a new 3,670 bhp MaK diesel engine, which made good sense as no further new tonnage was planned for the immediate future. Returning to service in March

The *Polarlys* received her new TFDS livery in 1979; she is seen here at the FrielenskaienTerminal, Bergen. *(Bruce Peter)*

A rare colour image of FFR's *Alta* (1950) seen on Coastal Express service off the Finnmark coast early in her career. *(Derek Longly)*

Photographed whilst berthed at Finnsnes in 1958, the *Alta's* sister ship *Sørøy* (1949) would also see plenty of relief work on the Coastal Express. *(Mittet)*

1982, the *Polarlys* was now the fastest ship in the fleet with a top speed in excess of 18 knots.

Her 40th anniversary on the Coastal Express was celebrated on 27th September 1992 at Bergen. By then she had travelled the equivalent of 130 times around the world – not bad for a 40 year old. The writing was on the wall for her as the new *Kong Harald* was scheduled to be delivered in June 1993. The *Polarlys* commenced her last round trip from Bergen on 6th June before going to lay up near Ålesund.

In late April 1994, the ship was sold to Mercy Ships, in conjunction with the inter-church organization Youth with a Mission, based at Lindale, Texas and renamed *Caribbean Mercy*. She was converted into a floating medical centre and eye clinic, mainly working in the Caribbean Basin, Central and South America and served in this role for almost a decade until June 2005. Her last known resting place (2012) was at Christobel, Panama, then very much a derelict hulk.

VITAL RELIEF

The post war renewal of the Coastal Express fleet was to take far longer than anticipated and it was over four years before this first phase of new vessels was completed. By 1949, with most of the Hurtigruten ships worn down by war, to bring them into line with the new regulations would be costly, given the short time that remained before their replacement. Equally, the remaining coal fired ships had become uneconomic to operate.

As the next trio of new builds from Aalborg Værft were not expected before 1951/52, both NFDS and BDS turned to Finnmark Fylkesrederi og Rutelskap (FFR) for help. With the Nordlandsbanen (Nordland Railway) still under construction, the three main coastal shipping companies based in Northern Norway, ODS, FFR, and Det Saltens Dampskibsselskab (SDS) had agreed to create a regional coastal service from Mosjøen to Hammerfest.

In 1946 FFR, who were based in Hammerfest, ordered two relatively large ships with good cabin space from Trosvik Mek Verksted, Brevik. At that time, with Mosjøen the northern terminus of the Nordlandsbanen, the three companies were advised not to become too heavily committed to the service as once the railway reached Bodø, that part of the route would be truncated.

The *Sørøy* was the first to be delivered on 1st September 1949, followed by her sister, *Alta,* in July of the following year. Both ships were representative of a new generation of Norwegian coastal steamer ships, good looking, compact and sturdy, their grey hulls set off by FFR's yellow, white and blue funnel colours. In appearance, they resembled a smaller version of the 'Italia-Båtene', which were then under construction at Ancona.

In October 1950, only three months after coming into service, the *Alta* was chartered to NFDS as a replacement for their *Kong Harald* on the service. Fifteen months later in February 1952, with the Aalborg new build *Håkon Jarl* ready to come into service, she was returned to FFR. She was then chartered again in the October of the following year by BDS to cover the absence of the *Nordstjernen*. Just to even things up, in 1958 VDS, the other main Coastal Express

Today, the Sørøy lives on as ***RTS Sindbad***, a training ship based at Port Rashid, Dubai. *(Uwe Jakob)*

An excellent study by Schrøder of ODS' slightly larger **Barøy** (1952) which was also saw regular Coastal Express service. *(STFM)*

operator, chartered the *Alta*, whilst their *Lofoten* was out of service.

The *Sørøy* had a number of short term charters to both to NFDS and BDS, as well as in 1951 being chartered by the Kings Bay Kull Compani as a replacement for the *Lyngen* on cruises between Tromsø and Svalbard.

After the tragic sinking of Det Stavangerske Dampskibsselskab's *Sanct Svithun* in October 1962, the *Sørøy* became one of the temporary replacements continuing to work regularly on the Coastal Express until DSD's new vessel, the *Kong Olav,* was delivered in 1964.

These versatile sisters became the victims of the vast improvements in the road network and the growth of air travel that the 1960s brought to the Nordland and Troms regions. In December 1965, the *Sørøy* was sold to become a Government floating training ship, based in Trondheim, being renamed *Skule*. The *Alta* continued in service until 1967 when she was sold to the Maritime Co-

Operative Shipping Association Ltd, Suva, Fiji. After rebuilding and the installation of air conditioning at Kaarbøs Mek, Harstad, she was renamed *Tui Lau* and put into service around the Fiji Islands. It would not be a long career as on the 25th October 1968 the *Tui Lau* grounded on a reef about 120 nautical miles from her home port of Suva and sank.

In 1981 the *Skule* (ex *Sørøy*) was transferred to the Østfold Fylkeskommune and renamed *Østfold*. In 1991 she became the *Glommen,* being resold in July 2003 to become a private residence moored at Oanes, near Stavanger. Less than a year later, in May 2004, she was purchased by Reef Line/Zambesi Shipping of Dubai and renamed *RTS Sindbad*. In partnership with the Australian Institute of Marine Education, the ship was totally refurbished for use as a training vessel and based at Port Rashid, Dubai. Kept in immaculate condition she continues to serve today.

In June 1951, ODS ordered their ship for the new regional

SDS'coastal vessel **Salten** was almost continuously on the Coastal Express during the late 1950's and early 1960's. *(Author's Collection)*

After the loss of the **Nordstjernen** in 1954, BDS used their new cruise ship **Meteor** from January 1955 to cover until a new **Nordstjernen** was ready some 13 months later. Seen here at Svolvær. *(Nordland Museum)*

coastal service from the Drammen Shipyard, Trondheim. Delivered on 21st February 1952, the *Barøy* (700 gross tons) was very similar to the *Sørøy* and *Alta*, with two continuous decks and superstructure amidships and aft. She had a passenger certificate for 250 persons and cabin accommodation for 26 in first class and 24 in second class. Her engine was a standard 870 bhp 6-cylinder Atlas Diesel which gave a 13.5 knots service speed. The *Barøy* was equipped with radar, echo-sounder, electric log and radio telephone, while part of her forward hold was refrigerated. The ship cost 4.3 million kroner which was twice the original price quoted!

She had only completed a couple of round trips on the Mosjøen to Hammerfest route when BDS chartered her for Coastal Express service until their new *Polarlys* was ready. In spite of her small size, she acquitted herself well, being highly manoeuvrable when berthing. On 4th September ODS returned to the service and the *Barøy* became the permanent fourteenth member of the fleet. For the first time in its history, the Coastal Express became a daily service between Bergen and Kirkenes.

Such was her success that in December 1955 the ship was lengthened by 30 feet, somewhat spoiling her looks but significantly increasing her capacity, returning to service on 29th April 1956. Her place, in the meantime, on the Coastal Express was taken by SDS's *Salten*.

In 1963 the *Barøy* was sold on to Birger Svendsen & Sons, Fredrikstad for ferry services across the Skagerrak between Arendal, Lysekil and Marstrand, tapping into the tax free market. With car ferries taking over, the *Barøy* was purchased in October 1966 by the Government of the Gilbert and Ellice Islands, Pacific Ocean, renamed *Teraka* and converted into a training ship for young people. Sadly, her new career was relatively short, as after suffering major mechanical problems, she was condemned and scuttled near the Betio lighthouse, Tawara on 19th June 1973.

That same year (1951) Saltens Dampskipsselskap (SDS) too ordered their new and similar motor ship from Trosvik Mek, Brevik for delivery in March 1953. The *Salten* was deemed to be an ideal permanent relief ship, particularly during the off peak and winter months and was to serve in this role until 1964, including stints for NFDS (1953), NDS (1958/9) and then following the disaster which befell the *Sanct Svithun* for DSD before, in 1964, being placed on the summer service to Svalbard.

In the spring of 1967, the *Salten* was sold back to the Government to become an adult education training ship based at Grimstad, southern Norway. Renamed *Sjøkurs,* later in 1973, she was based at the Sørlandets Seafaring Skoleskib Instutition in Kristiansand. Two decades later in 1995, the ship was temporarily renamed *Sjøskole* for sale to the Ryfylke Steamship Company of Stavanger and later renamed *Gamle Salten*. Veteran ship enthusiasts in Stavanger restored the ship to her former glory and she has since

been officially granted 'Cultural Heritage' status.

In 2008, when it became known that Ryfylke were going to sell the *Gamle Salten* as they were taking on another veteran ship, local enthusiasts based in Bodø formed Saltens A/S in order to purchase her. Today, in addition to her Cultural Heritage work, she has regular charters, runs her own cruise programme and in between serves as a restaurant and hotel ship. Sixty five years old in 2018, the *Gamle Salten* is as good as ever!

Disaster came to the Coastal Express on 20th September 1954, when the *Nordstjernen* (1937) foundered in the Raftsundet, on her way north from Svolvaer to Stokmarknes with 204 passengers on board, striking rocks which ripped open her hull, flooding the cargo spaces and boiler room. The sudden ingress of cold water caused the ship's boilers to explode and the ship sank in 160 feet of water within 20 minutes. Five people lost their lives in the incident.

BDS immediately turned to their elderly North Sea steamer *Jupiter* (1915) as a temporary replacement. One of the largest ships to have served on the Coastal Express she was also one of the most comfortable and being a steamer did not suffer from vibration. However, she was extremely costly to operate and BDS sought to replace her at the earliest possible opportunity.

Fortunately their new cruise ship *Meteor* was almost complete at Aalborg and her arrival in January 1955 meant that the *Jupiter's* reign was to be short lived and by September had been sold on to the Epirotiki Steamship Navigation Co. Ltd, Piraeus, Greece for rebuilding as a cruise ship, being renamed *Hermes*. On 4 March 1960, whilst refitting at Piraeus, she was destroyed by a devastating fire.

Of more modest proportions than her predecessor, *Stella Polaris*, the *Meteor* (2,856 gross tons) was painted in the company's new cruising colours of white hull and superstructure and buff funnel with three white hoops. In essence she was a larger and more luxurious version of the *Nordlys* and *Polarlys*, but still with the ability to be able to call at many of the smaller ports denied to large cruise liners; in other words, ideal to serve on the Coastal Express in a relief capacity. Immediately put into service as from 22nd January 1955, she was replaced for the summer months by the *Jupiter* while she undertook eight cruises, five to Nordkapp, two to the Baltic and one to Svalbard.

Just over a year later, ahead of schedule, in February 1956, BDS took delivery of a new *Nordstjernen* which meant that the *Meteor* was now free to undertake a more extensive and worldwide cruising programme, only rarely appearing again on the Coastal Express. In 1971 the ship was also sold to Epirotiki of Greece, where she was completely rebuilt and renamed *Neptune* to operate cruises in the Aegean and Mediterranean, as well as frequently revisiting Norway. Her career ended in 2002 when the ship was towed to Aliaga in Turkey to be scrapped.

With the sale of the *Jupiter*, once again BDS was without a

FFR's *Ingøy* was built in 1950 at Drammen Mek, Trondheim and is viewed there prior to taking up service. At only 433gt she was probably the smallest ship ever to serve on the Coastal Express. *(Author's Collection)*

suitable relief ship and so during the *Meteor*'s overhaul in the winter of 1955/6 the company chartered the *Ingøy* from Finnmark Fylkesrederi (FFR) which was a case of going from one extreme to another.

A smaller version of the *Barøy* series, the *Ingøy*, was built by Drammen Mek, Trondheim in 1950. Designed as a combined cargo and passenger ship for local services around Finnmark, she measured a mere 433 gross tons and was only 135.3 feet in length.

As far as is known, the winter of 1955/6 was her only spell on the Coastal Express and a complete 13-day round voyage on board must have been quite a unique experience. In 1971 FFR sold her to Gardline Shipping of Lowestoft, who renamed her *Researcher*. Later, the ship was purchased by Sidney Sea Search of the Cayman Islands and in 1983 sold on to the South Carolina Wildlife & Marine Rescue Department who deliberately scuttled her to form an artificial reef.

NEW BUILDS ON THE BLOCK

On 24th February 1956, a month ahead of schedule, BDS took delivery of their new 15.5 knot *Nordstjernen* (2,149 gross tons) from Blohm & Voss of Hamburg as a direct replacement for their previous *Nordstjernen* (1937) which foundered in the Raftsundet in 1954. The ship was a near sister to the earlier *Nordlys* and *Polarlys*, the main changes being in the modified styling of the forward end of her superstructure and only having four lifeboats instead of the five (2 port, 3 starboard) on the earlier sisters. Berths were provided for 192 passengers, and her passenger certificate was for 410 persons on coastal services.

The flagship of the BDS Hurtigruten fleet, she had a class certificate for international waters which enabled her to sail to Svalbard as well as to undertake spring shopping cruises to Lerwick

in the Shetlands, which she did from 1976 to 1979, making no less than 16 North Sea crossings.

Under TFDS ownership as from September 1979, and with the next Coastal Express contract stipulating that the the route was now to be run with only 11 ships, the *Nordstjernen* was sent to the Mjellem & Karlsen Shipyard, Bergen in the winter of 1982-83 for a comprehensive modernisation in order to bring her into line with the new safety regulations. Her old B & W engine was replaced by a 3,600 bhp 8-cylinder MaK diesel which improved both economy and speed. The results were startling, as once considered to be the slowest of all the new motor ships, the *Nordstjernen* now had a top speed of over 20 knots. In addition, the cabins on the main deck were gutted and rebuilt, many with en suite facilities, reducing the number of berths from 192 to 179.

With a new *Nordlys* arriving in the spring of 1994, the *Nordstjernen* became the relief ship, although from late June to early September she found employment on weekly cruises between Tromsø and Svalbard. In September 1995, she again returned to full Coastal Express service replacing the *Ragnvald Jarl* until the new *Polarlys* arrived in April 1996.

Her busy pattern of summer cruises along the 'Long Coast' and to Svalbard (later extended to include Greenland), as well as covering for winter absences, set the pattern for the next decade. Granted Cultural Heritage status by the Riksantvikvaren, Norway's Directorate for Cultural Heritage, the *Nordstjernen* had a further NOK 10 million upgrade at Ibestad Mek, South Tromsø during the winter of 1999/2000.

On 16th March 2003, the ship undertook a special cruise to her birthplace, Hamburg, to celebrate the arrival of the *Midnatsol*, meeting up with the new ship at the mouth of the River Elbe and

BDS' new *Nordstjernen* departing Harstad on her maiden voyage in March 1956. *(Harstad Tidende Archive)*

The *Nordstjernen* (right) and *Håkon Jarl* are seen together in Bergen in 1978, can you spot the subtle differences? *(Author's Collection)*

cruising together to Hamburg. Between 1st and 9th June 2004 the *Nordstjernen* acted as an escort for the Norwegian Royal Yacht, *Norge*, which was visiting Caen in connection with the 60th anniversary commemorations of the Normandy landings.

With both the *Nordnorge* and *Nordkapp* on expedition voyages around Antarctica for the winters of 2005/6 and 2006/7, the *Nordstjernen* returned to Coastal Express service on a regular basis. In the summers of 2007 and 2008 the ship was used for short Svalbard cruises under the Spitsbergen Adventure banner.

Whilst many thought that the arrival of the expedition ship *Fram* in 2007, would see her retirement, the *Nordstjernen* continued to be a regular on the Coastal Express, in particular covering for the *Finnmarken* whilst she was on charter as an accommodation ship for workers on the Gorgon oil and gas field project, north west Australia during 2010-2012.

With the ship now 56 years old, 2012 was scheduled to be the *Nordstjernen's* swansong as new Solas regulations were said to

make made further upgrading financially prohibitive. Her last official classic round voyage on the Hurtigruten began on 11th March 2012 and ended at Bergen on 22nd March where she was replaced by the returning *Finnmarken*. The ship then sailed to the Fiskerstrand Shipyard near Ålesund for a temporary layup and refit before embarking on a final season of cruises around Svalbard.

Upon arriving at Bergen from her last Svalbard cruise on September 1st 2012, she immediately undertook a 45 day charter for CCB (Coast Centre Base) as a hotel ship at their Ågotnes oil rig maintenance facility, Store Sotra, near Bergen.

The *Nordstjernen* was then put up for sale and on 26th November 2012, the ship was bought by Indre Nordhordland Steam Båtlag, Bergen, before being transferred to the ownership of Vestland Rederi AS based at Totvastad, Haugesund, on 3rd December. In connection with the sale, she was protected as a national heritage by the Norwegian Directorate for Cultural Heritage (Riksantikvaren). Subsequently from the end of 2012 to July 2013, she underwent an

In TFDS funnel livery as from 1979 *Nordstjernen* looks very much in her element cruising around Svalbard. *(Bjørn Andersen Collection)*

The **Nordstjernen**'s wheelhouse gives a wonderful glimpse of days gone by. *(Uwe Jakob)*

The cosy Panorama Lounge on board **Nordstjernen**. *(Uwe Jakob)*

extensive restoration in Gdansk, Poland, with her funnel now repainted in the old black and white BDS colours. Her new owners market her as both a hotel ship and for charter cruises. Since 2015 Hurtigruten have chartered her back for their explorer cruises around Svalbard each summer, so she still continues to be in active Hurtigruten service!

Both VDS and NFDS also ordered new ships in 1954 to replace their oldest steamers, in VDS's case, the *Finmarken* which dated from 1912. Although they would have preferred to order their new ships from a Norwegian yard, the prices the latter were asking were far too high, so in the end Blohm & Voss of Hamburg were awarded the contracts for two similar ships.

However, both the new *Finnmarken* (note the spelling) and the *Ragnvald Jarl* for NFDS (2,189 gross tons), differed radically from the new BDS ship, *Nordstjernen,* which Blohm & Voss were also building at the same time. They had been designed with the engine room located towards the stern, which improved the trim as well as providing space for more cabins as the amidships dining room was no longer divided by a funnel casing. With a passenger certificate for 585 on coastal voyages, there were berths for 67 first class and 142 second class travellers. The two forward holds had a total capacity of 21,830 cubic feet but cargo handling equipment on the foredeck was still of the traditional boom and derrick type. Whilst the 2,960 bhp 10-cylinder MAN diesel could produce a service speed of 16.6 knots, the engine could be reversed, which when combined with the variable pitch propeller, made it possible for the stern to be swung to port or starboard when moving astern.

Their radical appearance took a lot of people by surprise and there was a good deal of adverse comment. The superstructure above boat deck level was aluminium, reducing weight so offering

The **Nordstjernen** now sporting Hurtigruten funnel colours departs Molde in May 2011. *(John Bryant)*

Today, totally revamped and back in her original livery and looking immaculate, the magnificent **Nordstjernen** is photographed off Lyngen. *(Joachim Kohler)*

greater stability with the bridge deck being one full deck higher. Both were excellent sea boats, very practical, easy to keep clean and functional, but many found it hard to get used to the squat streamlined funnel astern and the midships mainmast.

Delivered to VDS on 29th May, with Captain Oscar Carlson as Master, the *Finnmarken* called at Oslo on a promotional visit before sailing on her maiden Coastal Express voyage on 8th June 1956.

The formal merging of VDS and ODS into Det Ofotens Vesteraalens Dampskibsselskab (OVDS) in January 1988 meant new funnel colours. The loss of the attractive VDS livery of blue band with white rings meant that she never quite looked the same again.

After 37 years of service, with the imminent delivery of the new *Richard With* in December 1993, the *Finnmarken* was laid up but in a bold move, OVDS agreed to allow the ship to become an integral part of the new Hurtigruten Museum at Stokmarknes. Funding was secured in 1997/98 and after 6 years of inactivity on 3rd May 1999, the *Finnmarken* was sent under her own power to the Kaarbø shipyard at Harstad, where her hull was sandblasted and repainted. On 14th June with Captain Sten Magne Engen in command, she sailed for Stokmarknes where he was able to order 'finished with engines' for the very last time. Two days later the ship was lifted ashore and placed adjacent to the Hurtigruten Museum in time for

The **Finnmarken** (1956) at Harstad preparing to go southbound in July 1975; note her squat streamlined funnel. *(Mike Bent)*

The merging of VDS with ODS to become OVDS meant fresh funnel colours for *Finnmarken*, seen here departing Tromsø in June 1988. *(Sigmund Krøvel-Velle)*

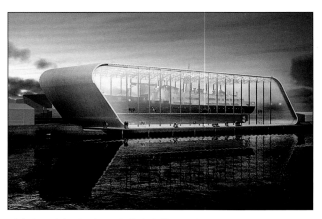

It is hoped that by the end of 2019 *Finnmarken*, as the largest land based museum exhibit in Norway, will be permanently enclosed inside this futuristic structure. (*Hurtigrutemuseet*)

its opening on 4th July 1999 making *Finnmarken* the largest land based museum exhibit in Norway. Some twenty years on, as from the end of 2019, a futuristic glazed structure will fully enclose the ship thus ensuring her preservation in a unique environment for all to enjoy for many years to come.

The new *Ragnvald Jarl* for NFDS was a direct replacement for her 1942-built namesake, which by now was too slow for the Coastal Express service. Delivered on 24th July with Captain Paul Holm as her first Master, the *Ragnvald Jarl* was not quite an identical twin to the *Finnmarken*, since the dining room on the promenade deck, occupying the full width of the superstructure, was without alleyways on either side. There were also differences in interior decoration and furnishings.

In the autumn of 1967, the *Ragnvald Jarl* returned to Hamburg for a thorough overhaul. The interior was refurbished and her engine

converted to use heavy fuel oil, the ship gaining the reputation of being the most economic on the route. Sixteen years later, this time in autumn 1983, the ship received another major refurbishment at Mjellem & Karlsen, Bergen, costing NOK 12 million in which the hull was sandblasted and the engine totally rebuilt with a new cylinder block and liners. The two lounges were merged, 12 new cabins built and others rebuilt with private shower and toilet. Overall this greatly reduced cabin capacity from 205 to 144.

For the spring of 1984 the *Ragnvald Jarl* was fitted with experimental lightweight satellite communication terminals and data recording equipment as part of the Prosat project to improve satellite communication technology. In the higher latitudes the elevation of the European Space Agency's Marecs satellite was very low, only 14 degrees above the horizon in Trondheim and close to zero degrees at Nordkapp, so a Coastal Express ship was ideal for testing the

NFDS' *Ragnvald Jarl* powers away northwards, it could be a bumpy ride given the conditions. *(Bruce Peter)*

The **Ragnvald Jarl** looks diminutive in the floating dry dock as she undergoes a wintertime refit. *(Hurtigrutemuseet)*

An August 1975 image of **Harald Jarl** and **Midnatsol** at the Festningskaien, Bergen. *(Mike Bent)*

technology under extreme conditions.

With the ship transferred to TFDS in August 1989, the *Ragnvald Jarl's* distinctive NFDS red band on its funnel disappeared forever. In what seemed to be a surprise move, in August 1995, TFDS sold the *Ragnvald Jarl* to Rogaland Sjøaspirantskole, Stavanger, who renamed her *Gann* and replacing the previous ship of that name, the old *Finmarken* of 1912. Based at Hundvåg near Stavanger, the vessel combined the role of training and cruise ship, operating in summer between Stavanger and Nordkapp and occasionally venturing to Svalbard as well. In March 2007, the ship was replaced by the *Narvik* of 1982 (also renamed *Gann*) but was quickly purchased for a similar role by Sørlandets Seilende Skoleskibs Institution, based at Kristiansand. Renamed *Sjøkurs*, the ship is still in active service today.

Building on their experience with the *Ragnvald Jarl* NFDS placed

a further order for new tonnage, with the *Harald Jarl* being launched at Trondhjems Mek on 29th January 1960 and delivered some five months later. Whilst basically of similar design to the *Finnmarken* and the *Ragnvald Jarl,* the architects had responded to the criticisms and produced a beautifully well proportioned ship with a combined mast and funnel positioned just aft of amidships. In addition, the placing of the lifeboat davits above and clear of the boat deck was much more pleasing aesthetically and these improvements were to be further developed in the next three Coastal Express ships to be delivered in 1964.

Costing 14.7 million kroner, the ship was much larger than the previous two vessels, measuring 2,568 gross tons, and 20 feet longer at 286.8 feet, with a certificate for 652 passengers. The decor was of a high standard with Arnstein Arneberg's architect Find Nilson responsible for the interior and artist Kåre Espolin Johnson for

In 2007 the ex **Ragnvald Jarl** was sold again to Sørlandets Seilende Institution, Kristiansand, and renamed **Sjørkurs**. Viewed here about to pass under the Gruenental Bridge whilst transiting the Kiel Canal in 2017. *(Juergen Braker)*

Harald Jarl is now named *Serenissima* for Premier Cruises and is probably in her best condition ever since new. Seen departing Portsmouth in May 2014. *(John Bryant)*

Nostalgia! The Chief Engineer of the *Lofoten* checking that all is running well in the engine room. *(Ørjan Bertelsen/Hurtigruten)*

the art-work. The ship's navigation equipment for the first time included an auto-pilot. The *Harald Jarl's* prime mover was a 3,450 bhp 5-cylinder Burmeister & Wain diesel which enabled a trials speed of 18.3 knots.

On 23rd June 1960, the *Harald Jarl,* now the NFDS's flagship, under the command of Captain Christian O. Odegaard, departed from the Festningskaien, Bergen on her maiden voyage to Kirkenes, the ship replacing the *Sigurd Jarl,* which was the last of their steamships in service. In 1962, 569,579 passengers were carried on the Coastal Express, the highest number ever and a record still unbroken some 60 years later.

After 41 years of service, with new ships on the way, the *Harald Jarl* set out on her last round trip on the Coastal Express on 9th October 2001 after which the paintings and murals by Kaare Espolin Johnson were carefully removed for transfer to the new *Trollfjord.* Apparently the paintings were valued at NOK 15 million, while the ship was advertised for sale at just NOK 10 million! The *Harald Jarl* was in fact to spend the winter at the Fosen shipyard, serving as an accommodation ship.

In July 2002, the *Harald Jarl* was sold to Elegant Cruises Inc., who renamed the ship *Andrea.* A major refurbishment was undertaken at Uddevalla (Sweden), where large areas of the

Is this 1964 or 2018? It matters not, *Lofoten,* with her original funnel livery restored, departing Ørnes with Bodø as her next port of call. *(Uwe Jakob)*

lounges including furniture were renewed and cabins upgraded. The Andrea was marketed as a 4-star cruise ship, with a capacity for just 106 passengers, advertising a series of cruises around the Baltic Sea and Norwegian coast, Adriatic and even Antarctica. However, in 2009 she was laid up at Vranjic, Split in Croatia and it wasn't until April 2012 that she was sold to the Moscow based Volga Dream Cruises for further service. Now renamed *Serenissima* (and operated by Premier Cruises, Mariehamn, Finland), she is kept busy being chartered to several operators (including Noble Caledonia) for cruises around the Mediterranean, Black Sea, British Isles and Norway.

MORE ADDITIONS TO THE FLEET

In February 1962, VDS, ODS and SDS signed a contract with the Aker group for three new ships, all to be built to the same basic design based on the *Harald Jarl*. The Vesteraalen and Ofotens ships were to be constructed simultaneously at Akers Mek, Oslo, whilst the contract for the Stavanger vessel was given to their Bergen shipyard. The loss of the *Sanct Svithun* in October 1962 would be deeply felt by the latter company.

For VDS, it was now time for their 1932-built *Lofoten* to be replaced and on 7th September 1963, a new *Lofoten* (2,597 gross tons) was named and launched by Asbjørg Bergsmo of Stokmarknes, her predecessor having been renamed *Vågan* the previous autumn. Powered by a 3,325 bhp 7-cylinder Aker built B & W diesel, she attained a speed of 17.49 knots on trials. The ship had berths for 53 first class and 180 second class passengers, with several of the cabins being interchangeable between classes. Relatively few however, were en-suite.

Late on the evening of 5th March 1964, under the command of Captain Svein Eriksen, the *Lofoten* slipped out from the Festningskaien, Bergen, on her maiden voyage. By mid-June her two near sister ships *Kong Olav* and *Nordnorge* would also enter service. Whilst built to the same specification, each company would mark their individuality particularly in the design and placement of the funnel, the *Lofoten* having a very squat funnel which was not dissimilar to the *Harald Jarl* in profile.

In October 1980, the *Lofoten* was sent to Aalborg Værft, Denmark for reconfiguration into a one-class ship, the former second class dining room being converted into four large cabins. At the same time her engines were thoroughly overhauled. Only five years later, the ship was again back at Aalborg for further upgrading with many of the cabins being rebuilt with en suite facilities, reducing her berth capacity to 223. She even received a blue hull, but this was to be a short-lived experiment.

In January 1988 with VDS and ODS formally merging into Det Ofotens Vesteraalens Dampskibssellskab (OVDS), the *Lofoten* was now registered in Narvik and sported the Ofotens funnel logo.

The *Lofoten* photographed at Trondheim in OVDS funnel colours which she wore from January 1996 until 2006. *(Bruce Peter Collection)*

The entrance lobby on board *Lofoten*. *(Ørjan Bertelsen/Hurtigruten)*

Lofoten's Saloon Deck Lounge. *(Uwe Jakob)*

There was another funnel livery change for *Lofoten* in 2006 with the formation of Hurtigruten ASA. She is seen here in March 2014. *(Miles Cowsill)*

However, the ship was not to remain long under this new ownership as on 1st September 1988, she was sold for NOK 20 million to Finnmark Fylkesrederi og Rutelskap, based in Hammerfest. FFR had been invited to join the Hurtigruten consortium and the *Lofoten* was to be their contribution; as a consequence it meant another funnel livery change. The company had big plans for the future but in late 1991 with first of the 'new generation' ships being built at Stralsund in Germany, they were not able to secure the necessary funding for a further new build for the route. As a result, on 1st January 1996 the *Lofoten* was sold back to OVDS for NOK 35 million and formally handed back a month later.

In January 2001, the *Lofoten* was granted 'Cultural Heritage' status by the Riksantvikvaren, Norway's Directorate for Cultural Heritage, although with three further new ships on order it appeared that her Coastal Express days were numbered. OVDS, however, made plans for her to operate shorter cruises working out of Bodø in summer and in winter to act as a relief vessel. Replaced by the new *Finnmarken* on 2nd February 2002, she was sent for a thorough upgrade at Kaarbø Verft, Harstad, which included new fire safety systems.

In both 2005 and 2006, the *Lofoten* made 7-day cruises from Bergen each April, May and September, taking in Stavanger, Hardangerfjorden and Flåm before returning south. For the summer peak she sailed further north up the Helgeland coast to Bodø, which then became the base for another series of weekly cruises in the Nordland and Lofoten areas. For the summer of 2007 the *Lofoten* was based in Svalbard offering week long cruises under the marketing banner of 'Spitsbergen Explorer'. Since then with the sale of two of the 'mid generation' ships, the *Lofoten* has permanently returned to the Coastal Express service and is much loved by a loyal crew and discerning clientele. Today, in tribute to her longevity, she once again sports her old VDS funnel livery and offers her guests special experiences which enhance the heritage of the service, recapturing the spirit of her early days in the 60's. Long may she continue!

The new DSD ship, now a direct replacement for lost *Sanct Svithun*, was constructed at Akers Mek, Bergen, being named *Kong Olav* at her launch by Randi Gowart-Olsen on 15th November 1963. She was the first Coastal Express ship to be built there since the *Midnatsol* of 1910. Although of the same basic design as the two consorts being built for VDS and ODS at Oslo, there is no doubt that this 16.5 million kroner vessel was probably the finest looking of all the first generation post war motor ships, beautifully set off by the well proportioned dummy funnel (in the distinctive Stavanger colours with its three red bands) aft of the bridge deck. The engine exhaust was discharged through the mainmast located aft. The ship was to be the first route steamer to have a bow thrust (400 hp Liaaen) unit to aid manoeuvrability on and off the berths. Passenger comforts were not forgotten as the ship boasted heaters on the saloon windows to prevent icing-up.

The *Kong Olav* was formally handed over to DSD at Stavanger on 11th April 1964, receiving a personal visit from King Olav of Norway himself. The *Kong Olav* proved to be a very popular ship on the route and, as with the *Lofoten* and *Nordstjernen*, was involved in the Svalbard Express programmes which ran from 1968 until 1982, together with spring mini cruises to Aberdeen in the 1970s.

Financial difficulties, together with the ship being based away from her home port, meant that the Hurtigruten operation was becoming less pertinent to the Stavanger region and as a result, on 11th April 1978 the *Kong Olav* was sold to VDS for NOK 17.5 million (a million more than the ship had cost as new). The dummy funnel was repainted in the VDS blue, white and black livery but only a decade later in 1988, with the merger of the Vesteraalen and Ofotens companies completed, the *Kong Olav's* funnel received the OVDS colours of red and white with a blue symbol on a yellow background.

By the mid 1990s with three further 'new generation' ships to be constructed at Ulsteinvik, the *Kong Olav's* tenure on the Coastal Express was rapidly coming to an end. On 30th April 1997, after 33 years of service, the ship docked in Bergen for the final time to be replaced by the new *Nordnorge*.

The vessel was immediately sold to a hotel group, the Andaman Club Co Ltd, Bangkok, Thailand for use on 2/3 day cruises for divers and tourists based on Phuket and as a hotel/casino ship off the Similan Islands in the Andaman Sea (Burma). The project was hit by the Asian financial crisis of 1998, which had major consequences for tourism. The *Kong Olav* was laid up at Ranong, in the Southern Thailand Anchorage. She remains there as an unwanted derelict hulk, though some of its furniture and fittings have now found their way for use and display in a local restaurant and bar.

For Ofotens (celebrating their golden jubilee), permission to build a full-size Coastal Express ship to replace their reliable but diminutive *Barøy,* was welcome and deserved news. Built at Akers Mek, Oslo, at a cost of 17 million kroner, the ship was named *Nordnorge* (2,611 gross tons) on the 1st February 1964 by Randi Bratteli, wife of the then Transport Minister. Similar in design to her two consorts, the ship was marginally the largest member of the fleet.

On the evening of 11th June 1964, under the command of Captain H Waagønes, the new Coastal Express flagship sailed from Bergen on her maiden service. On the southbound voyage she diverted to make a special call to her home port and headquarters of ODS, Narvik, which had not been served by the Coastal Express since 1953.

With the introduction of the *Nordnorge*, the route now had 13 similar ships of the same standard capacity and a 15-knot service speed available, bringing both reliability and stability to the whole operation for almost the next two decades. It would not be until the winter of 1982/3 with the new *Narvik* entering service that there was any significant change. The *Nordnorge's* crew transferred to the new ship, whilst the crew from the now retired *Håkon Jarl* transferred to the *Nordnorge*.

Upon the arrival of the *Nordkapp* in April 1996, the *Nordnorge* was laid up at Narvik prior to being sold to Templeman Inc of Panama and renamed *Worldlink*. Sold on again to Universal Enterprises, Mali and renamed *Island Explorer*, the ship was revamped at Piraeus for service as a dive cruise vessel based around the Maldives. Furnishings and cabins were upgraded (56 de luxe) and air conditioning installed throughout. The outer deck was extended aft complete with swimming pool and the hull was painted white with a blue stripe. It looked as if her long-term future was assured, but on 19th December 2005, whilst based at Ari Atoll, Kandholadhow, the decision was taken to sell her for scrap. In early January 2006, with a ride crew on board and under her own power, the ship departed the Maldives for Alang, India and demolition.

THE SVALBARD EXPRESS 1968 – 1982

Regular sailings to Svalbard were revived after a gap of twelve years in the summer of 1951 with the *Lyngen* from TFDS carrying on from where she had left off in 1939, making just three round trips. By the middle of the decade there were six departures from Tromsø each summer connecting with the Coastal Express service. With each trip designed to last eleven days, the actual day of departure varied in order to minimise turn-round time and maximise ship usage. Calls were made at Bjørnøya, Isfjord (where a tender was used to drop off supplies), Longyearbyen and Ny-Ålesund before

The *Kong Olav* in her original DSD funnel livery arriving at Trondheim, June 1975. *(Mike Bent)*

Now a VDS ship *Kong Olav* in the arctic ice whilst on the Svalbard Express service. *(Riksarkivets Norge)*

A sad image taken in May 2017 of the *Kong Olav*, derelict some thousands of miles away at Ranong, in the Andaman Sea. *(Captain Jan-Olav Storli)*

The graceful lines of Ofotens *Nordnorge* are shown to good effect in this image; note the cars on the fo'c's'le. *(Trond Carlson /Hurtigrutemuseet)*

sailing north to Magdalenefjorden and the edge of the polar ice pack around 80°N.

Both freight and mail traffic to Svalbard had been on the increase, mainly from those working at the European Space Research Organisation's satellite-tracking station at Ny-Ålesund and at the Norsk Polarinstitutt's base. Despite poor weather and adverse ice conditions the popularity of the Svalbard cruises grew, encouraging TFDS and Aftenposten (Norway's largest newspaper) to form in 1965, 'Nordpolhotellet', as a means of enticing visitors to spend longer on Svalbard. One of the old mining companies' buildings was rented and refurbished as a hotel, with a total of fourteen bedrooms. The hotel's staff travelled north on *Lyngen*'s first sailing of each summer, returning home on the last one. In 1965 there were eleven round trips with 796 passengers carried with that summer being noted for its warm weather, at Ny-Ålesund the temperature reached the comparatively dizzy heights of 18°C.

The following year, 1966, the service was maintained by the *Sørøy* and *Salten,* under charter to TFDS with nine round trips and 781 passengers carried. The hotel project was less successful and only used by around 60 guests, closing for good at the end of the season.

It was the Coastal Express consortium as a whole which came to the rescue, being granted permission by the Norwegian Government to develop the Svalbard market for themselves. Each company would contribute its most recent ship for fortnightly summer cruises from Bergen, returning thirteen days later and calling only at the major ports between there and Honningsvåg. The first sailing of this new venture was taken by the *Harald Jarl* and departed from Bergen on 8th June 1968. By 1970, no fewer than 11 weekly departures were on offer and made possible by bringing forward the southbound Hurtigruten departure service from Trondheim by four hours from 16.00 to 12.00, resulting in a lunchtime arrival in Bergen the following day. Instead of lying over at Bergen for 26 hours the ship could then set off again late that evening.

The 'Svalbard Express', as it was marketed, had a holiday cruise element about it, the vessels became one-class and fares were inclusive of all meals, only varying according to the grade of cabin required, the forerunner of today's Hurtigruten cruise operation. From Honningsvåg the schedule had to be more flexible, depending on cargo requirements, weather, ice and the cruising ranges of the individual ships. The itinerary generally offered passengers a glimpse behind the Iron Curtain at the Russian mining town of Barentsburg, together with visits further north to Magdalenefjorden and the polar ice beyond 80°N.

Following the withdrawal of the *Erling Jarl* in 1980 the service became fortnightly only but the decision to reduce the Hurtigruten fleet from twelve to eleven vessels from the winter of 1982/3 made the 'Svalbard Express' no longer viable. The last sailing was appropriately taken by the *Harald Jarl* which arrived back at Bergen on 28th August 1982.

It was not the end for the Svalbard experience as we shall see later, although its revival was a long time coming.

Berthed at a snowbound Havøysund, *Nordnorge*'s stern looks a little bit the worse for wear. *(Arnulf Husmo/Mittet)*

CHAPTER SIX

Fresh Thinking

The next five-year contract commenced on 1st January 1963 and anticipating the introduction of three new ships into service, a revised timetable was devised based on a standard service speed of 15 knots. This was inaugurated on 16th September 1964 by the *Polarlys* with her 23.45 departure from Bergen. For the first time in its history, the Coastal Express was had a fleet of ships of almost standard size and standard performance characteristics, with a mere fifteen years between the oldest and most recent vessels. It appeared to be an almost perfect solution. Or was it? No more new builds were to appear for another 18 years.

In spite on the introduction of the new ships and the revised timetable, the overall performance the route that year was not good. Freight levels were down and there was increasing competition from rail, air and bus services. Increases in tariffs were more than offset by heavy expenditure. The contract had to be extended on a year-by-year basis as negotiations faltered each time over future subsidisation levels.

By 1972 inflation was rampant. Freight tariffs were up by 12.5%, passenger fares up by 10% and diesel fuel up by no less than 95%. In 1974, in order to save fuel and bring down costs, the summertime northbound service would run directly from Havøysund to Honningsvåg, rather than going via Skarsvåg and Nordkapp.

There was better news at nearby Berlevåg, where the new Hurtigruten quay, protected by two massive breakwater arms, opened in late November 1974. Tenders were no longer needed to land passengers or cargo.

The completion of the Nordlandbanen linking Trondheim and Bodø in 1962 was anticipated to have a marked influence on the future development of transport services along the stretch of coastline between the two ports. In theory, travellers in a hurry would opt for rail rather than sea whilst express freight trains carrying fresh fish in refrigerated vans would draw some of this traffic away from the coastal ships. In reality, the Nordlandbanen failed to live up to expectations and generated a deficit of 554 million kroner in 1976 which had to be covered by the State. Even though freight rates and passenger fares were higher on the Coastal Express for the same distances, in terms of real costs, transportation by sea still remained cheaper than rail.

The post war years had seen a huge expansion in domestic airline services. SAS had inaugurated daily flights from Oslo to Bodø, Tromsø and Kirkenes and by the mid-1970s there were over thirty commercial airline companies in Norway vying for custom. Some of the flight schedules were more akin to a bus service, the Trondheim to Bodø service, for example, having intermediate stops at Sandnessjøen, Brønnøysund and Namsos. Fares were competitive with the Coastal Express and certainly not excessive when compared with rail. The air services captured most of the business travellers who hitherto had used the coastal steamers and even light mail now went by air.

The transition of freight from lift-on/lift-off shipping services to road hauliers was positively encouraged with roll-on/roll-off ferry services being introduced on those fjord crossings which were too broad to be bridged. The result was far greater flexibility and drastically reduced journey times.

As dependence on local and coastal shipping services dwindled, ship operation altered rapidly. Pallet loading, using forklift trucks driven on and off vessels via doors in the sides of the ship's hull were becoming the norm. Turn-round times in port were reduced, as were labour costs. Larger unit loads, beyond the capacities of pallets and fork lift trucks, were lifted aboard by electrically powered cranes. Over the next two decades this new technology became almost universal, which put the current Hurtigruten ships at a distinct disadvantage; their cargo handling operation was outmoded from the day they were built.

Whilst car ferry services were now dominant across Europe, the

Tromsø based Troms Fylkes Dampskibsselskap (Troms County Steamship Company) house flag.

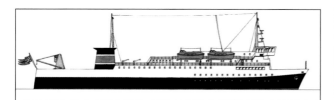

Norwegian Ministry of Transport's (Samferdselsdepartment) 1978 proposal for the next generation of 'hurtigrute' ships. *(Mike Bent)*

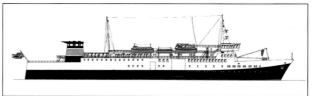

The Coastal Express Consortium's proposal. *(Mike Bent)*

Coastal Express fleet was only able to take a few cars or light vans, craned on and placed wherever space permitted on exposed foredecks. With some of the fleet now 25 years old it was not just a case of wear and tear as the overall standard of accommodation was now well below what could be experienced elsewhere.

In 1975, the companies were envisaging new ships of around 3,000 gross tons with berths for around 150 passengers and a service speed of 20 knots. A fleet of nine vessels of identical design and performance was being suggested, with a much-accelerated daily service. Whilst in the short term, the benefits were clear to see (uniformity and compatibility), in the long term it would have created the same major issues, since all nine ships would eventually require replacement almost simultaneously.

By May 1976, the Storting (Norwegian Parliament) appeared to be resigned to abandoning the route south of Bodø and providing a daily service from there to Kirkenes using just seven vessels. However, persistent lobbying convinced the Minister for Transport, Ragnar Christiansen, to change his mind. He announced that future transport policy would focus upon 'promoting those modes and routes which had the lowest social costs' (i.e. not on purely economic grounds). The Coastal Express along with other coastal shipping services were once again back in favour.

TOWARDS THE NEXT GENERATION

Two proposals were put forward in 1978: one from the Samferdselsdepartement (Ministry of Transport) and the other from the companies themselves. The latter's revised proposal was a for vessel of 3,000 gross tons, 360 feet in length with a service speed of 17.5 knots and a passenger certificate for 450 and berths for 200 persons.

The Ministry were looking at something around 30 feet shorter, a smaller deadweight capacity of 350 tonnes, a lower passenger certificate of 375 and berths for just 85 persons.

The Ministry's vessel would be equipped with a crane and a pallet lift for cargo handling, whilst the consortium's proposal would have also had a stern door, enabling her to accommodate all types of road vehicle.

By August 1979, it was agreed that the starting point for the definitive design of the new ships should be based on the companies' proposals. A working party was created under the

leadership of Ragnar Kobro, the administrative director for VDS. Four one-class ships were envisaged, with passenger certificates for around 400 and berths for 150 persons. The estimated cost per ship of between NOK 80 million and NOK 100 million escalated as the Gulf War caused oil prices to rapidly rise, fuelling general inflation, so that by November 1980 the cost per vessel had doubled to NOK 160 million. The decision was then made to only build three ships for which the State would provide 76% of the total building costs as well as an increase in the operating subsidy for the new ships.

For DSD, the post war value of the Coastal Express to the Rogaland and Jæren districts, of which Stavanger was the hub, had been on the wane. The ferry route to Bergen was now in the hands of fast craft and DSD's main activities more concentrated on local ferry and coastal cargo services. The *Kong Olav's* operation had become a financial burden for little return and so early in 1978, the ship was sold to VDS.

The sale triggered off another takeover when, amidst great secrecy, TFDS approached BDS with a view to purchasing their four Hurtigruten ships. In a similar position to DSD, the Bergen company felt that their resources could be better utilised in other areas of their business, namely the offshore oil industry. When the news was released on 24th January 1979 there was a storm of incredulity; where was the wisdom in the deal, paying NOK 32 million for four ships between 23 and 30 years old?

Over the next eight months BDS and TFDS worked together to run the four ships. On 30th August 1979 the *Nordlys* and *Polarlys* were formally handed over, followed by *Midnatsol* and *Nordstjernen* on 4th September. The jobs of the 250 or so crew members were all guaranteed. NFDS were also looking for a buyer for their *Håkon Jarl* and after negotiations with Saltens fell through, Ofotens purchased her for NOK 8 million on 17th January 1981. At the same time NFDS transferred its new Hurtigruten contract to ODS, whilst still continuing to operate the *Ragnvald Jarl* and *Harald Jarl*.

The wheel had turned full circle as for the first time since 1894, control of operations was with northern coastal companies. This new mix of operators promised fresh ideas and a greater commitment to maintaining the service. ODS, VDS and TFDS were in a much more suitable position geographically to understand and cater for the transport needs of communities in the far north. It was a new era and no doubt Richard With would have had a smile on his face.

The automatic folding gangway would make disembarkation so much easier. *(Author's Collection)*

The newly completed *Midnatsol* (1982) with its single white funnel on the starboard side gave it a rather unbalanced look. *(Ulstenvik Shipyard)*

The first day of January 1983 was a sad day in the history of the service as all on-board post offices were closed and the transport of mail by sea continued only where no alternative existed. On most of the ships the spaces formerly occupied by the mail rooms were converted into additional cabins, although on the *Nordnorge* a conference room was provided instead. However, in the mid 1990's the ships were once more allowed to fly the postal flag in recognition of the special status the Coastal Express has in Norway.

THE MID GENERATION SHIPS

On 22nd May 1982, Elisabeth Giæver, daughter of John Giæver, chairman of Troms Fylkes Dampskibsselskap named and launched the company's new 'mid generation' ship *Midnatsol* (4,131 gross tons) at the Ulstein Hatlø Shipyard, Ulsteinvik. The ship, unlike anything seen before, was in effect twice the size of her predecessor with about three times the cargo capacity.

The *Midnatsol* was a twin screw ship (a first for a Coastal Express new build), powered by two 3 200 bhp 16 cylinder 4T Bergen M/V KVM diesels, with twin rudders and two 401 hp Brunvoll SPT-VP bow thrust units to aid manoeuvrability. Designed with a service speed of 17.5 knots, the diesels were adjusted so that the ship could operate efficiently at the lower 15 knot service speed demanded by the timetable. Much use was made of floating floors and elastic mountings for both the main and auxiliary engines in order to reduce noise and vibration levels. The new ship had a certificate for 410 passengers with 181 berths in 86 en suite cabins all situated in the forward part of the ship and spread over three decks. Two decks above, on E Deck, there was a large panoramic observation lounge, whilst one deck below was a small dining room (which also doubled up as a conference room) together with other lounges. For the first time crew could enjoy a similar standard of accommodation to that provided for passengers.

After being laid up for two years, in 2005 *Midnatsol* was reactivated, re-entering Hurtigruten service as *Lyngen* and seen here off Molde in June 2007. *(Uwe Jakob)*

Sold in late 2007 to Lindblad Expeditions, *Lyngen* became their *National Geographic Explorer*, captured at Ipswich in May 2017. *(Stephen Waller)*

The Finnmarken or Forut Restaurant, on board the ex *Narvik*, now named *Gann*. *(Uwe Jakob)*

Cargo-handling equipment, including a 15 ton crane (with 18m reach) was to be found on the aft open deck which could take up to 22 standard TEU (20 ft) containers and/or covered palletised loads. Inside, on B Deck there was space for up to 40 vehicles. The storage rooms for perishable goods were on A Deck where there was also a large room (580 m³) for deep-frozen foods. With no provision for stern loading, cargo access to the ship was provided by large doors on the port side which meant that berthing would always be on this side. A new feature was the hydraulic gangway for passengers, making boarding and exiting the ship much more easy.

Extremely functional in design, the *Midnatsol* was hardly likely to win many plaudits. Her exhaust uptakes were concealed in a yellow painted box-like structure on the starboard side aft of the superstructure, giving the ship an unbalanced look. The company colours, of black, white and red bands were painted on the deck housing at the base of her mainmast.

On 26th November the *Midnatsol* was ready for her delivery voyage to Bergen, where she was escorted in by her predecessor, now renamed *Midnatsol II*. The contrast between the two could not have been more marked.

It was not long after her maiden voyage from Bergen on Sunday 5th December 1982 that the complaints came in; the new *Midnatsol* was just too small! The restaurant provision, with room for just 68 diners at one sitting, received the greatest amount of adverse comment as on busy days in the summer months, up to three sittings had to be provided. In an attempt to alleviate the problem during the autumn of 1983 the fixed bulkheads between the restaurants and adjacent lounges were replaced by moveable partitions to offer greater flexiblility.

The second of the trio of 'mid generation' ships, the *Narvik*, was built at Trondhjems Mek, and with Captain Peder Pedersen in

In 1988/9 *Narvik* and her two 'mid generation' class sister ships had their accommodation extended at the stern. Note the two funnels though one is a dummy. *(John Bryant)*

The *Gann* (ex *Narvik*) is photographed passing under one of Kristiansund's bridges. *(Uwe Jakob)*

A new *Vesterålen* in the final fitting out stage at Harstad in February 1983. *(Harstad Tidende Archive)*

command (formerly of the *Nordnorge*) she made her delivery voyage north to Narvik, the headquarters of Det Ofotens Dampskibsselskab (ODS). There she was formally named by Anne-Marie Pleym, for many years the booking manager of ODS, on 16th December 1982.

The following day, with most of her crew having been transferred from the *Nordnorge,* the new ship took over *Håkon Jarl*'s southbound Hurtigruten sailing from Harstad. Unlike the *Midnatsol*, she did not have an observation lounge on E Deck and there were a number of other detail differences in her design. Her funnel was painted in the company colours rather than being left blank.

Built at Kaarbø Mek, Harstad, VDS's new *Vesterålen* was the last

of the new ships to take to the water. Apart from her livery, the ship was practically a twin sister of the *Narvik* and was formally named on 16th February 1983, by Elsie Kobro at Stockmarknes.

When this generation of new ships was designed, the accent was still on the crane loading of cargo, albeit in containers or pallets. However, it became clear early on that this was a mistake and at the expense of passenger capacity needs. In 1987, a contract was signed with Motorenwerk, Bremerhaven to rebuild the ships, but before this happened the ODS/VDS merger took place on 1st January 1988, an upshot being that the *Vesterålen* lost her attractive blue, white and black funnel livery together with the distinctive blue

A fine view of *Vesterålen*'s deck layout, she is about to pass under the Nærøysund Bridge at Rørvik. *(Uwe Jakob)*

The **Vesterålen**'s Fyret Panorama Lounge is an ideal place to watch the world go by. *(Uwe Jakob)*

Pallet loading using forklift trucks was a great improvement over the old crane loading method. *(Author's Collection)*

stripe along her hull.

The *Midnatsol* was the first to be sent to Bremerhaven for a prefabricated passenger accommodation module to be fitted over the aft cargo deck. Two new funnel casings were constructed, one a dummy, which gave the ship a more balanced look. The restaurant was rebuilt with 68 new seats and in the new stern section there was a bar and lounge as well as further cabin accommodation with another 156 berths. Whilst this reduced her cargo capacity, the ship now measured 6,167 gross tons. The cost of this work was NOK 40 million. On 14th March 1988 the *Midnatsol* returned to service and whilst everyone agreed that the ship looked impressive, opinions were still divided as to whether she was, visually, an improvement.

In the October it was the *Vesterålen's* turn to be sent to Motorenwerk to have her new passenger accommodation module and panoramic lounge installed at a cost of 45 million kroner. Twelve months later, in the autumn of 1989, the *Narvik* went to Germany for a similar rebuild, bringing her into line with her consorts.

In 1995, further refurbishments to all three ships were carried out at the Haugesund Mek Shipyard, bringing improvements to the reception area, dining room and some of the cabins as well as providing for the growing conference market.

In February 1998, the *Vesterålen* became involved in a project with the Stavanger Research Institute, investigating climatic change and global warming. The ship carried a water temperature sensor, fitted at a depth of four metres on her hull which took measurements every five minutes, recording the precise location via GPS.

Towards the end of 2000 TFDS ordered a new ship to replace the 18-year old *Midnatsol* although she was still relatively young in terms of previous Coastal Express longevity. In January 2003 the ship was renamed *Midnatsol II* and three months later, on 15th April,

On a beautiful sunny morning at Trondheim **Vesterålen** is preparing to depart southbound for Bergen. *(John Bryant)*

The Narvik based OVDS (Det Ofotens Vesteraalens Dampskibsselskab) house flag.

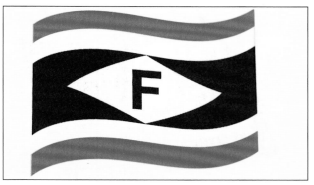

House flag of FFR (Det Finnmark Fylkesrederi og Rutelskap), Hammerfest, which became part of the Hurtigruten consortium from 1988 to 1996.

she arrived at Bergen for what was thought to be her last time in service. Meeting up with her successor, the contrasts were just as great as when she met the 1949 built *Midnatsol* in 1982. The *Midnatsol II* sailed north to lay up at Fiskerstrand Verft, Ålesund and was advertised for sale. Two years of inactivity followed until June 2005, when in a surprising announcement it was revealed that she would return to service. Following a refit at the Rissa shipyard near Trondheim, the ship sailed to Lyngseidet, where on 24th of September she was renamed *Lyngen* after that region of northern Norway. The ship returned to service the following day, standing in for the *Trollfjord* which had been chartered for a special cruise. With both the *Nordkapp* and *Nordnorge* away on Antarctic cruises as from the end of September, the ship became the regular reserve vesel.

By late 2006, the *Narvik's* time on the Coastal Express was coming to an end and having been chartered to Norsk Hydro as an accommodation vessel for three weeks in October, the *Narvik* was purchased by the Young Christian Seafarers Association (Rogaland Secondary Sjøaspirantskole), Stavanger as a training ship for young mariners. Upon delivery on 21st February 2007, the ship was renamed *Gann,* replacing the previous ship of that name, the ex *Ragnvald Jarl.*

In October 2007, the *Lyngen* was sold to Lindblad Expedition for conversion into an exploration ship. After major work at both Gothenburg and Las Palmas on 8th August 2008 she was renamed *National Geographic Explorer* and successfully continues in her new role today.

The *Gann* (ex *Narvik*) was in the news in late April 2010 when in the wake of the disruption caused to flights from the erupting Eyjafjallajökull volcano in Iceland, she ferried stranded tourists from Stavanger to Newcastle.

Whilst it may have seemed somewhat surprising that her two sister ships should have been withdrawn (rather than the older *Lofoten* and *Nordstjernen*), the *Vesterålen* has continued in service. In February 2008, she was sent to the Fredericia Shipyard in Denmark to have stabilisers fitted, a sure sign that she would remain on the Coastal Express for some years to come.

THE NEW GENERATION

The introduction of the three 'mid generation' ships into service in 1983 marked the beginning of the end of the old order as far as the Coastal Express companies were concerned. In that year BDS merged with the Sandefjord based Kosmos A/S. A year later, in October 1984, NFDS was purchased by Norcem, who in turn, took Kosmos under their wing as from April 1995. At the same time, large amounts of shares in VDS were being purchased by ODS, so it was no surprise that on 1st January 1988 the two companies merged to form Det Ofotens Vesteraalens Dampskibsselskab (OVDS). The latter company then sold the *Lofoten* to Finnmark Fylkesrederi (FFR) for NOK 20 million, bringing in another new company to the table.

With Troms Fylkes Dampskibsselskap (TFDS), Det Stavangerske Dampskibsselskab (DSD) and Saltens Dampskibsselskap (SDS) joining forces in 1988 to become RoNoTro, the whole ball game changed once more when, a year later, this new company acquired both BDS and NFDS from Kosmos. The operation was now entirely in the hands of three companies based in northern Norway.

The continued dissatisfaction with the three 1982/3 ships, and in particular their passenger capacity, had resulted in the 1988/89 rebuilding programme, which the companies had to finance themselves with no aid from the State. It was clear that if the Coastal Express were to survive then it would have to markedly expand its tourism rôle and to provide suitable facilities and experiences accordingly. Passenger numbers had fallen from 384,700 in 1978 to 277,000 by 1982. The rebuilding work had arrested the decline, but as we shall see, it was not until the arrival of the 'new generation' ships that any new growth began to be experienced.

Entering the final years of the 20th century, the 1950s built ships were in urgent need of replacement and a whole decade had passed since any new ships had been ordered. 1990 would be the last year that the Coastal Express served Alta and Gamvik (the most northerly port on the route) as in future all sailings for the latter port would now call at Mehamn. In June, the Storting agreed that the Coastal

Norwegian Coastal Voyage
advertising from the 1980's
onwards

Express should receive State support of NOK 1.875 billion spread over twelve years. NOK 1.3 billion was to be used for new builds and the remainder as an operating subsidy. Skip Consulting A/S, Bergen, in consultation with the companies, was charged with developing a specification for new ships which would have cruise liner standards of comfort. More than 20 shipyards were then invited to tender, both in Norway and abroad.

Six proposals were short listed, with the German specialist cruise ship builders, Meyer Werft at Papenburg, being successful. The actual building contract with options for two sister ships was awarded in March 1991 to Volkswerft GmbH, Stralsund, based in the former East Germany. Their bid of NOK 400 million per ship being NOK 100 million less than the lowest tender from any Norwegian shipyard.

THE STRALSUND TRIO

The three 'new generation' ships were to set new standards both in terms of passenger comfort and interior design as well as that of expectation, ushering in a new era in Coastal Express history. One class ships, operated by a crew of 55, they had spacious communal areas, a panoramic observation lounge, a cafeteria, a restaurant, bars and conference rooms. Certified for 691 passengers in coastal service, there were 490 berths in 230 en suite cabins (all with heated bathroom floors) of which 212 have outside views. Saunas and a fitness room are provided as standard.

The ships (11,204 gross tons) load and unload on the port side using forklift trucks through a large side portal which has a 5-ton pallet lift, with a double width hydraulic passenger gangway adjacent to the main reception area.

Each had three fridge/freezer units with a total volume of 880m³ and a cargo deck capacity of 1,500m³. The 600m² car deck could

Kong Harald's attractive foyer area on Deck 4 as originally built. *(John Bryant)*

The arcade which leads aft to *Kong Harald*'s restaurant. *(John Bryant)*

Kong Harald in TFDS livery speeding southwards from Havøysund in May 2006. *(John Bryant)*

Kong Harald, as she looks today, departing Tromsø en route for a late evening call at Skjervøy. *(Uwe Jakob)*

initially accommodate up to 45 cars. The engines were 2 six-cylinder four-stroke Krupp MaK DM 6 C M552 diesels with a total output of 12,228 hp, each driving a propeller giving a top speed of 20 knots. In addition, to the two 1,075 hp Brunvoll bow thrust units these were the first Hurtigruten ships to be equipped with active-stabilizer fins.

The first of the 'new generation' of ships to be completed was the *Kong Harald* for TFDS and formally named at Stralsund by Hjordis Opseth, the wife of the then Transport Minister, Kjell Opseth, on 25th June 1993. Although named after the King of Norway, other eminent Norwegians were honoured on board, including the Fridtjof Nansen bar and the Roald Amundsen café.

On 2nd July, the vessel arrived at Trondheim to help celebrate the route's 100th anniversary. The *Kong Harald* immediately sailed to London for a promotional visit before beginning her maiden voyage from Bergen on 6th July 1993, replacing the 1952 veteran *Polarlys*.

In January 1995 the ship was sent to Bremerhaven for her guaranteed warranty docking and at the same time received a 1,200 hp azimuth thruster which was installed at the stern to improve manoeuvrability.

In all her time in service the *Kong Harald* has only rarely been in the news, although 2011 was very much the exception to the rule. On 18th April, during a period of extremely low spring tides, the ship with 227 passengers on board touched the bottom whilst en route from Ålesund to Molde, suffering a 50 metre gash and holing two

tanks on the starboard side. Later, over the Christmas period storm force winds whipped up by Hurricane Dagmar forced the ship to seek shelter at Trondheim for four days until conditions had eased.

Intended as the centenary vessel, the *Richard With* was the second of the Stralsund trio appropriately taking the name of the route's founder, though she was not handed over to OVDS until 22nd November 1993. The ship was named by Aashild Haugen on 19th December 1993 and put into service the following day from Harstad, replacing the *Finnmarken* (1956). Internally, much of the attractive art work on board was produced by the Harr family based in Harstad, Eva, Jan and Karl Erik; the latter's 'Trollfjordslaget' (commemorating the 'Battle of Trollfjord' in 1890), on Deck 4 was quite stunning. Today, she also boasts two Jacuzzis on Deck 6.

The *Richard With* was used for a variety of charters particularly in her early years, generally in the off peak winter months. In August 1997, the ship had the distinction of being the first of today's Hurtigruten vessels to sail into Geirangerfjord as part of its northbound Coastal Express summer timetable, setting a precedent which all ships follow today.

The *Nordlys* (Northern Lights or Aurora Borealis) was the last of the ships built by Volkswerft GmbH, Stralsund, being handed over to TFDS on 16th March 1994. Internally, local Norwegian artists created a distinct feel on board the ship, its art, décor and colour palette all inspired by the Northern Lights, together with a wide use of fine textiles and attractive wood and brass fittings. Upon the handover, the *Nordlys* sailed directly to Copenhagen, Denmark for a promotional visit before doing the same at Hamburg, Germany.

Kirsti Kolle Grondahl, the first female President of the Storting, formally named the ship in Oslo on 22nd March, before she sailed across the North Sea via Stavanger to Newcastle and London, becoming the first Coastal Express ship to berth at both the Tyne Bridge and Tower Bridge respectively. Returning to Bergen on 4th April, the *Nordlys* set out on her maiden Hurtigruten voyage that same evening, replacing the *Nordstjernen*.

With OVDS and TFDS experiencing some financial constraints in 2002/2003, both the *Richard With* and the *Nordlys* were sold, not to dispose of the ships but to increase the company's available capital. At the request of Nordnorge Sparebank (which had provided loans for its construction) on 2nd December 2002, the *Richard With* was sold to Kystruten KS, Fosnavåg, for NOK 375 million. The sale of the *Nordlys* followed on 30th April 2003 for NOK 400 million to a consortium including Kirberg Shipping KS, Bergen (50%) and Den Norske Bank (44%). Both vessels were then leased back as bare boat charters on 15-year agreement with buy-back options after 10 and 15 years or a further additional five years on market terms. OVDS and TFDS (today Hurtigruten AS) would each be responsible and pay for the operation, insurance and all necessary ongoing maintenance of the ship. In October 2017 it was announced that Hurtigruten AS would now buy back both the *Richard With* and *Nordlys*.

In bad weather with high winds on the morning of 6th January 2009, the *Richard With* experienced great difficulty when trying to berth at Trondheim and made heavy contact with the quayside resulting in damage to one of the propeller shafts as well as a

The Polar Restaurant on board *Richard With*. (John Bryant)

Part of Karl Erik Harr's stunning Battle of Trollfjord 1890 art work on board *Richard With*. (John Bryant)

Richard With is still in her original OVDS livery when arriving on a southbound service at Harstad, May 2006. (John Bryant)

A stern three quarter view of *Richard With* at Harstad's northbound Hurtigruten berth. *(John Bryant)*

watertight stern gland, partially flooding the engine room. As a precaution, the 153 passengers were taken off the ship via a fire tender ladder. Later in the day, the leakage from the starboard stern tube was stopped and the bilge pumps were able to empty the engine room of water. The *Richard With* was then sent to Bredo Werft at Bremen for repairs, not returning to Hurtigruten service until 5th April.

Worse was to befall the *Nordlys* on 15th September 2011, as whilst approaching Ålesund, a serious fire in the engine room killed both the Chief Engineer and a young motorman apprentice on his first voyage. Twelve others were hurt, two sustaining serious injuries. The ship managed to berth at Ålesund and all 207 passengers were taken off the ship while some of the 55 crew remained on board to assist with fire fighting operations. Owing to a loss of electrical power, the stabilizers, which were deployed at the time of the incident, did not automatically retract as they should have done when the ship's momentum was below 6 knots. The starboard stabilizer hit the quayside and was forced back into the hull allowing water to ingress. The ship tilted almost 22 degrees and there was some danger that she would capsize. A temporary concrete seal was eventually put in place and the vessel pumped free of water. Both the

ship's passengers and media were full of praise for the way in which the crew and Hurtigruten had handled a very difficult situation.

The ship was then towed to Fiskerstrand Verft, near Ålesund, where the shipyard was later contracted to undertake the repairs. The *Nordlys* returned to Hurtigruten service on 28th March 2012, some 8 days later than scheduled, leaving southbound from Tromsø.

The subsequent AIBN report indicated fatigue cracks in fuel pipes were the cause and remedial actions were immediately taken to ensure that this did not reoccur. In November 2013 came a fresh international directive regarding stability of vessels in which ships would now need to install new bulkheads to prevent water ingress. These modifications and further stability directives have led to reductions in car capacity for the *Nordlys*, her two Stralsund built sister vessels and more recently the three 'New Generation MKII' ships.

NEW GENERATION MK II

Such was the success of the first three 'new generation' ships that in 1994 TFDS and OVDS were each given permission to order another ship, the contract being awarded to the Kleven shipyards at Ulsteinvik with each vessel to cost around NOK 500 million. Although of similar specifications (11,386 gross tons; 123.3 metres long,

The *Nordlys* passing under the Raftsundet Bridge. *(Enok Leonhardsen/Hurtigruten)*

The Tromsdalen mountains make a fine backdrop for the *Nordlys* at Tromsø, locally known as the 'Paris of the North'. *(John Bryant)*

A classic study of *Nordkapp* at Trondheim waiting to depart northbound. *(John Bryant)*

speed 18.5 knots, 691 passengers, 481 berths, and up to 45 cars etc.) there were differences between the two ships both externally and in terms of the propulsion unit chosen, the *Nordkapp's* being the more conventional two MaK 6M552C diesels as fitted to the first three ships in the series.

The *Nordkapp*, built for OVDS, was launched on 18th August 1995 but it was not until the 23rd March of the following year that the ship's Godmother, Queen Sonja, performed the naming ceremony, reportedly needing three attempts to persuade the champagne bottle to break. Similar in lay out to the Stralsund trio, the ship was fitted out to an extremely high standard with paintings by the renowned Harstad painter, Karl Erik Harr (whose work was also to be seen on the *Richard With*), adorning the ship's communal areas with pictures of traditional Lofoten fishing boats and other sailing motifs. Later upgradings to the ship would include four mini suites, two Jacuzzis and an internet café.

Just over a week later on 2nd April, with Captain Edgar Solstad in command and 146 round trip passengers on board, the *Nordkapp* departed from Bergen on her maiden voyage. The ship replaced the *Nordnorge* (1964) which was sold for cruises around the Maldives.

The success of the new *Nordnorge's* Antarctic voyages, begun in 2002, prompted OVDS to deploy the *Nordkapp* in the Southern Hemisphere for the 2005/6 and 2006/7 seasons, the *Nordstjernen* taking over her Hurtigruten schedule each winter. Meeting up in Antarctica with her newer sister ship, the *Nordnorge,* was always one of the highlights of these cruises.

On 30th January 2007, whilst off Deception Island, part of the South Shetland archipelago, on an Antarctic cruise, the *Nordkapp* ran aground, causing a 600mm gash in her hull. The incident made the news headlines on account of the possible environmental consequences, as whilst transferring light marine diesel fuel from the ruptured tank to an undamaged one, it was estimated that some 500 to 750 litres had escaped into the ocean.

The *Nordkapp* was refloated and anchored in Whalers' Bay, to await the arrival of *Nordnorge*, which was eight hours' sailing time away. A transfer of the 294 passengers and eight of the crew took place the next morning, the *Nordnorge*, which already had 243 passengers and her own crew of 76, sailed for Ushuaia in Argentina, arriving there just over two days later.

Although the damage to the *Nordkapp* was relatively limited and the vessel could have returned to Argentina, it was deemed prudent to make temporary repairs in situ, as well as accept the help of divers from a British naval vessel who also made a thorough inspection of her hull.

With the arrival of the expedition ship, *Fram,* for the 2007/8 season, the *Nordkapp* has returned to full time service on the Coastal Express and has not visited Antarctica since.

Learning from the experiences gained from their Stralsund built *Kong Harald* and *Nordlys*, TFDS wanted their third new build of the 1990s 'new generation' class to have increased flexibility and in consequence, greater earnings potential. Three main areas were pinpointed: conference facilities to be increased in size and versatility; cargo areas redesigned so as to be some 30% larger and the engines and their management systems to afford greater

The original arcade décor on board *Polarlys*. *(Uwe Jakob)*

Polarlys' Lokalen Café on Deck 4. *(Uwe Jakob)*

economy and flexibility.

Building commenced at Ulstein Verft, Ulsteinvik on 1st February 1995 and just over 13 months later on 23rd March 1996 the ship was named *Polarlys* by Ann-Kristin Olsen, the Governor of Svalbard, and was the third Coastal Express vessel to bear this name. On the same day at the nearby Kvaerner Kleven Shipyard, the new OVDS ship *Nordkapp* was being named by Queen Sonja of Norway.

A short promotional cruise followed along Norway's west coast before the *Polarlys* sailed across the North Sea to visit both Shetland (Lerwick) and Orkney (Kirkwall) before on 17th April, under the command of Captain Arne R. Erntsen, the ship began her maiden voyage from Bergen.

Her interior décor, designed by architect Finn Falkum-Hansen, was outstanding, the *Polarlys* becoming known as 'a ship with a soul', or 'the elegant jewellery box' with her mixture of polished mahogany and brass, glasswork, paintings, marble carvings and sculptures.

The main propulsion system differs from the *Nordkapp*, consisting of four 9-cylinder Ulstein Bergen 4-stroke diesel engines connected in pairs on each propeller shaft; a BRM 9 in front and a KRG 9 to the rear. The engines were designed to run in various combinations depending on needs, providing better fuel economy. A

Another image from Harstad taken in 2002 with *Polarlys* sporting her TFDS funnel livery. *(Uwe Jakob)*

Berlevåg is one of the more remote ports but also the noisiest as each night two Hurtigruten ships meet exchanging raucous greetings. Here *Polarlys* is saying goodbye to the departing *Nordnorge* in May 2013. *(John Bryant)*

Polarlys approaching Havøysund with the world's most northerly windfarm as the backdrop. *(John Bryant)*

unique feature of this is that the ship does not have auxiliary generators as both propulsion and electricity supply comes from the power plant. At the stern the ship has a 1,200 hp azimuth thruster to aid manoeuvring. Used on its own in an emergency, it can generate a speed of up to 7 knots. Rarely in the news, the *Polarlys'* reliability record has been second to none since she entered service.

In late 1995 permission was given for a sixth 'new generation' ship, an identical sister to the *Nordkapp*, to be built at the same Kværner Kleven shipyard, though the cost had now risen slightly to NOK 511 million. The new *Nordnorge* was delivered to OVDS on 14th March 1997 and registered in Narvik. Her interior furnishings very much reflected an Art Nouveau/Art Déco influence graced by watercolours from the Lofoten artist Dagfinn Bakke as well as by Johanne Marie Hansen-Kone and Ellen Lenvik. On 20th March, the *Nordnorge* was formally named by Sissel Marie Rønbeck, Minister of Transport and Communications, having technically entered service the previous day.

For the winter of 2002/3, the ship undertook a series of eight cruises from Argentina and Chile to the Antarctic. In that first season 1,700 passengers were carried, so the programme was repeated for the 2003/4 winter, with positioning cruises being advertised, enabling passengers to join for all or part of the voyage. For the winter of 2003/4 no fewer than 2,400 passengers were carried, with almost every cruise being fully booked.

The popularity of this venture led to OVDS in 2004/5 increasing the range of itineraries, including a 18-day cruise itinerary from Ushuaia, embracing Antarctica, South Georgia and the Falklands, with visits to some of the old Norwegian fishing and whaling stations.

In the following years other variations were on offer, one encompassing a 43 day cruise between Hammerfest (the northernmost town in the world) and Ushuaia (the southernmost), a

Panorama Lounge on board **Nordnorge** in its original form. *(Uwe Jakob)*

Nordnorge's Vestfjorden Lounge and Bar was a very cosy place in which to relax. *(John Bryant)*

The flags are flying on Norwegian National Day (17th May) with **Nordnorge** on the berth at Kirkenes. *(John Bryant)*

On a beautifully warm summer's day *Nordnorge* powers away from Stokmarknes towards the Raftsundet, Trollfjord and the Lofotens. *(Uwe Jakob)*

The 'Millennium Class' ship *Finnmarken* in her OVDS funnel livery seen berthed at Trondheim in 2005. *(Uwe Jakob)*

mere 9,915 nautical miles, whilst the northbound spring return was extended into a Baltic cruise before returning to Bergen. The winter of 2005/6 was the first time the *Nordnorge* and *Nordkapp* were based together in the Antarctic.

On 23rd November 2008, the *Nordnorge* was involved in the rescue of all 100 passengers and 54 crew from the sinking expedition ship, *Explorer*, after she had made underwater contact with an iceberg off King George Island.

The *Nordnorge* was joined by the new explorer ship *Fram* for the 2007/8 Antarctic season, from both Ushuaia and Punta Arenas. Having in April 2008 returned to her normal Coastal Express duties, at the end of that summer season she was chartered to Aker Solutions ASA as an accommodation ship in the Adriatic for the offshore oil industry, returning to Hurtigruten service in late 2009.

The *Nordnorge* and her crew become national celebrities in June 2011 when the ship was used by Norwegian Television Company NRK for their 'Hurtigruten minutt for minutt' live transmission of the whole 134 hours of a Hurtigruten journey from Bergen to Kirkenes. The weather was almost perfect, thousands of people came out to see her arrive and depart at each port. Millions watched the broadcast and NRK2 which normally attracts only four per cent of Norwegian viewers, became the country's biggest TV channel with a 36 per cent share. It proved to be a great advertisement for Hurtigruten.

THE MILLENNIUM CLASS

Following agreement with the Ministry for Transport and Communications towards the end of 1999 both OVDS and TFDS made plans for further new ships, designed with the wider cruise market in mind. This series of ships would become known as the 'Millennium Ships'. Whilst OVDS would design what would be essentially an enlarged version of the 'new generation' vessels, TFDS, for whom there would be two ships, would bring a fresh approach.

OVDS returned to the Kværner Kleven, signing a NOK 750 million contract on 10th May 2000 for a new vessel with intention of replacing their *Lofoten*. By 24th January 2001, the first keel modules were in situ sourced from Norway, Poland and Lithuania; the cabin modules would arrive later from Finland. On 9th February 2002 the new *Finnmarken* began her sea trials and on 4th April, the new OVDS flagship was formally named at Ulsteinvik by Torhild Skogsholm, the Minister for Transport and Communications.

The *Finnmarken* (15,530 gross tons) was, for a few weeks, the largest (and is still the longest) ship in the Coastal Express fleet with 40% more deck space than any other previous vessel. Her four Wärtsilä engines comprise of two 5,630 hp 9L32 diesels linked to two six-cylinder 3,780 hp W6L32 diesels, giving a total output of 18,820 hp. The propulsion system is designed to run in five different modes, using both diesel-electric and conventional mechanical transmission, enabling one main engine to drive both propellers simultaneously. The *Finnmarken* has two 1,370 hp Brunvoll bow thrust units and at the stern a 1,650 hp Ulstein azimuth pod which can rotate 360°. Blohm & Voss active fin stabilisers are installed amidships. The ship has three fridge/freezer rooms with a total volume of 790m³ with loading through the large side doors on the port side, where there is also deck space for up to 35 cars.

Certified for 1,000 passengers on the coastal route the *Finnmarken* has 628 berths spread over 285 cabins, which includes 18 mini suites and 14 large suites. All cabins boast heated bathroom floors, refrigerators, safes, telephones and televisions. The ship is tastefully decorated in the Art Nouveau style, with many local artists contributing drawings, watercolours, oil paintings, lithographs and sculptures. In addition to the panoramic observation lounge, bars, restaurant, cafeteria, shop and conference facilities, the ship also boasts an outdoor heated swimming pool, two Jacuzzis, a fitness centre, solarium and a hairdressing salon.

After the naming ceremony, the *Finnmarken* embarked from Bergen on a two week round Britain cruise before visiting Hamburg, Copenhagen, Oslo and Stavanger. On 20th April 2002, she began her maiden voyage from Bergen.

In 2005, the *Finnmarken* was adapted to become an emergency hospital ship, the Norwegian Armed Forces being responsible for specifications, design and construction as well as covering the costs. With the ship having her own water plant, electricity and waste management systems, it means that she can be at sea for long periods of time.

On 6th October 2009, Hurtigruten announced that the *Finnmarken* had been chartered for 18 months as an accommodation vessel in connection with the Gorgon Oil and Gas field project off the coast of Western Australia, a contract worth around NOK 697 million to the company. The ship was to be manned by key Hurtigruten deck and engineering officers, together with locally sourced crew. Extensive adaptation work, including painting her hull all-white, was carried out between November 2009 and March 2010 at the Westcom Shipyard, Ølensvåg, before the ship sailed via Cape Town to Fremantle for final preparations.

Sorely missed by both passengers and employees, it came as welcome news when it was announced in October 2011 that the ship would be returning to Hurtigruten in 2012. After a major refit and refurbishment in Singapore, including her 10-year survey, the *Finnmarken* returned via the Cape of Good Hope to Bergen, where on 16th February she began her first Hurtigruten voyage for over two years, taking over the *Nordlys'* roster until 22nd March after which she replaced the veteran *Nordstjernen*.

Hot on the heels of OVDS's announcement, TFDS signed a NOK 715 million contract on 1st June 2000 with Fosen Mek, Rissa

In 2010 *Finnmarken* was chartered for 18 months as an accommodation vessel for the Gorgon Oil and Gas Field off Western Australia. She was repainted in all white and is seen here arriving at Freemantle. *(John Kent)*

The popular Babette's Café on board *Finnmarken*. *(John Bryant)*

Finnmarken's very comfortable Brotoppen Panorama Lounge. *(John Bryant)*

Calmness personified, **Finnmarken** is beautifully reflected in the water at Kirkenes. *(Steffen Nuspel/Hurtigruten)*

A powerful image of **Finnmarken** departing Nesna for Sandnessjøen. *(Uwe Jakob)*

(Trondheim) for a further ship; the *Trollfjord* was to be very different both in design and construction.

On 18th April 2001, work started on the keel at Bruces Shipyard, Landskrona, Sweden, with the hull being launched six months later on 10th October and then towed to Rissa for completion. The ship was handed over to TFDS on 13th May 2002, some six weeks later than scheduled, meaning that an inaugural cruise programme had to be cancelled. The formal naming was performed by Kari Bremnes, a well-known Norwegian singer/songwriter from Svolvaer with the *Trollfjord's* maiden voyage, under the command of Captain Tormod Karlsen, from Bergen some five days later.

The *Trollfjord* (16,140 gross tons), is technically the largest in the fleet, has a certificate for 822 passengers with 654 berths in 305 cabins of which 19 are suites and five have a balcony. Her crew of 74 share 53 cabins. Spread over nine decks, with a five deck atrium as its centrepiece, the ship has two conference rooms, restaurant, cafeteria, bars, shop and lounges including a twin level panoramic observation lounge. The décor on the *Trollfjord* is full of cool blues and contemporary images of northern landscapes, so is very much a winter ship. On her top deck is a small pool and jacuzzi, with the water at a constant 37°C which is quite an experience especially when the outside temperature is twenty degrees below zero! Valuable paintings by artist Kaare Espolin Johnson, previously displayed on board the 1964-built *Harald Jarl*, now grace the *Trollfjord* and are to be seen on Deck 8.

Wärtsilä was also the choice for the *Trollfjord's* main engines, being two 9-cylinder 4-stroke W9L32 diesels each with an output of 8,280 kW, giving a service speed of 18 knots. Two Ulstein Aquamaster azimuth pods which can be rotated 360°, eliminating the need for a rudder, are also fitted. Forward are three 1,200 kW Brunvoll bow thrust units. The ship conforms to all the latest

The spacious Saga Hall Restaurant on board *Trollfjord*. *(Rory Coase/Ships in Bergen)*

Trollfjord's split level Panoramic Lounge *(Rory Coase/Ships in Bergen)*

In TFDS funnel livery *Trollfjord* is photographed off Åndadsnes near Molde in June 2005. *(Terry Whiffen)*

Trollfjord accelerating away from Harstad on a northbound service in March 2017. (*(John Bryant)*

A three quarter stern view of the powerful looking *Trollfjord* as she approaches Rørvik. (*Uwe Jakob*)

environmental regulations, emits minimal CO_2 gases as well as being quieter and near vibration free.

Since entering service the *Trollfjord* has proved to be an ideal choice for short-term charter work and cruises including, in her earlier years, an Easter circumnavigation of Britain, as an exhibition/hotel ship for the Winter Festival Week in Narvik and later for the Northern Lights Festival in Tromsø, together with a special centenary celebration voyage for Kaare Espolin Johnson, the artist, some of whose works adorn the ship.

The construction for TFDS of a new *Midnatsol* (the fourth Coastal Express ship to be so named), indicated the likely demise of one or more of the 1982 'mid generation' vessels after a relatively short working life on the Coastal Express. A follow-on order was signed with Fosen and immediately after the hull of the *Trollfjord* had departed from Bruces Shipyard, Landskrona, Sweden, work on the keel began, so that by the 26th April 2002, the *Midnatsol's* hull was ready for launching and towing to Rissa for completion.

Whilst the *Midnatsol* is a sister ship to the *Trollfjord*, she differs in that she can also be used as a hospital ship in case of war, crisis or disaster. The Norwegian Navy contributed NOK 6.5 million towards the cost of her construction, so that part of Deck 10 could be equipped as a full-scale hospital with beds for up to 200 patients, an intensive care centre, and four operating theatres. The ship has her own water and electricity supply and waste management systems on board, which means that she can be at sea for long periods of time. The lifts are sufficiently large enough to take hospital beds and the vessel also has a helideck. The car deck too can be converted into field hospital manned by up to 70 doctors and nurses.

The *Midnatsol* has a passenger certificate for 1,000 passengers, 178 more than her sister ship, with 648 berths spread over 304 cabins, of which 15 are suites (some with a balcony) and seven mini-

A rare view of TFDS' **Midnatsol** under construction in 2002 at Fosen's Rissa Shipyard near Trondheim. *(Herman Jelstad)*

It a long way down to the bottom! **Midnatsol's** stunning atrium lift shaft. *(Rory Coase/Ships in Bergen)*

In TFDS livery Midnatsol makes a sharp turn off the berth at Ålesund; next stop Molde (Aage Schjølberg)

Only in summer can the northbound Coastal Express be photographed at Risøyhamn in daylight; here *Midnatsol* approaches the berth. *(Uwe Jakob)*

Midnatsol about to pass under the bridge at Brønnøysund. *(Helmut Fiedler/Hurtigruten)*

Midnatsol's new tender deck was well used on her winter cruises to Antarctica in the winter of 2017/18. *(Miles Cowsill)*

suites. Her restaurant, located aft on Deck 5, can accommodate no fewer than 335 guests at one sitting. Large glass expanses allow light to permeate throughout the ship, enhancing the warm pastel yellows, oranges and russets, which together with complementary wood tones, reflect the aura of the midnight sun.

The ship was formally handed over TFDS on 14th March 2003, sailing two days later from Trondheim, cruising both the Geirangerfjord and Sognefjord, before making her way down to Stavanger and on to Hamburg for the naming ceremony. At the mouth of the River Elbe, she was met by the veteran *Nordstjernen* (built at Blohm and Voss, Hamburg), the ships sailing in tandem up river to the German city. The official naming ceremony, on 23rd March, was performed by Rut Brandt in a gesture to reflect the importance of the German market to the Coastal Express. Her sailing back to Norway was via the Keil Canal, Copenhagen and Oslo; two further promotional visits to the Shetlands followed, before on 15th April 2003 she was ready to make her maiden voyage from Bergen.

In August 2004, the NRK (Norwegian Broadcasting Corporation) began filming a 20 episode series entitled 'Coastal 365', depicting life on board the *Midnatsol* affording excellent publicity for the route. In January 2006 the *Midnatsol* was chartered to act as a hotel ship (based at Savona) for the duration of the Turin Winter Olympics, offering on the way cruises with calls at Hamburg, Rotterdam, Portsmouth, Lisbon and Barcelona.

Very much viewed as the flagships of today's Hurtigruten, both the *Midnatsol* and *Trollfjord* have continued to be used on numerous trade charters and special cruises, often organised by Hurtigruten's agent in Germany, Norwegische Schiffahrt Agency (NSA). This reflects the popularity Hurtigruten has in that country, which provides around half of the round trip passengers on the Coastal Express route. More recently in 2014 the *Midnatsol* as part of a special 'Heart of Norwegian Lapland' cruise circumnavigated Magerøya (the large island which on which Nordkapp (North Cape) is situated, an experience last done by Coastal Express ships some forty years previously in 1974.

Today, showing her versatility, under Hurtigruten's enhanced 'Explorer' programme the *Midnatsol* now spends September to April on cruises to South America and Antarctica. A special tender deck was constructed on Deck 3 (the car deck) to enable embarkation safer and easier for guests going on shore expeditions by rib boat. During her time away she is replaced on the Classic Voyage from Bergen to Kirkenes by the newly acquired *Spitsbergen*.

CHAPTER SEVEN

Towards Hurtigruten AS

NEW AGREEMENTS

Whilst the Coastal Express has long played a vital role in the commercial life of Northern Norway it is acutely aware of the ever changing dynamics as other transport means impact on their services and viability.

As the millennium drew near, an influential body of opinion argued that after 2001 it should no longer be necessary to continue with subsidies, suggesting that a more market-oriented solution of splitting the route into smaller sectors would enable the Hurtigruten companies to better bear their own costs. However, politicians in the Storting believed that the value of the service to Norwegian society was central, as a transport infrastructure and as a driving force for both regional development and tourism with particular spill-over effects on the commercial life of Nordland, Troms and Finnmark. A totally free and market-oriented situation would change the structure of transport provision negatively for the communities along the coast, resulting in fewer calls and a more focused cruise activity.

Whilst the Coastal Express cannot bear its own costs, the amount of subsidy given by the Norwegian Parliament for each passenger

could not be said to be excessive when compared to that given for alternative transport facilities. Their decision was for the Coastal Express to continue with the support package to subsidise passenger transport rather than cargo or tourism.

The 2001-2004 agreement made provision for both OFDS and TFDS to order further new ships and as a result, by the time the new *Midnatsol* was delivered in 2003, the fleet consisted of nine modern post 1993 ships and two modernised ships from the 1980s (the *Midnatsol* of 1982 having been withdrawn). In addition, the Coastal Express companies were guaranteed the concession by the state for the Bergen-Kirkenes route until 2010.

When new discussions began again in early 2004 over the next contract the old arguments appeared once more. Some potential bidders suggested that it would be more cost effective if the service was reduced to four days per week and operated in two sections, Bergen to Tromsø and Tromsø to Kirkenes. If this proposal were to be accepted there would be major repercussions for tourism and classic round trip passengers with all change at Tromsø. Not surprisingly, the

Fram was Hurtigruten's first purpose built explorer ship; she is seen here at Hamburg in May 2007 on her maiden cruise. *(Uwe Jakob)*

only submission was a joint one from OVDS and TFDS, with final agreement being reached on 5th November. The new contract would run from 2005 to 2012, with the companies receiving an annual subsidy of NOK 237 million (NOK 1.9 billion in total) and the service would continue to be daily, in full, from Bergen to Kirkenes.

NEW BERGEN TERMINAL

In the meantime the opening of the new NOK 240 million Hurtigruten Terminal at Nøstebryggen, Bergen on 1st March 2005 allayed any fears that the service south of Trondheim might one day be withdrawn. For nearly a century until the early 1980s the Coastal Express ships had berthed at the Festningskaien, in the Vågen at Bergen, before moving to the Frielenskaien Terminal, which was rather tucked away out of sight away from the daily city centre landscape. The new Nøstebryggen terminal is close to the city centre and opposite the attractive residential area of Nordnes where good views can be obtained of the ships arriving and departing.

MERGER 2006!

In the meantime OVDS and TFDS were actively pursuing a merger of the two companies, reaching agreement on 1st November 2005 and formally sanctioning it two weeks later. Workforce places would be shared between the two companies on a 50/50 basis, whilst any job losses resulting from the merger would also be shared 50/50. Shareholder approval was obtained on 19th December 2005, followed by the Monopolies and Mergers Board giving its consent two months later. From the 1st March 2006, the Coastal Express would be operated by a single company, the Hurtigruten Group (today known as Hurtigruten AS), with its head offices initially based in Narvik but since 2013 in Tromsø.

The tasteful Qilak Observation Lounge on board *Fram*. (John Bryant)

Fram's Expedition Suites are luxurious in the extreme. (Øyvind Grønbech/Hurtigruten)

Many major cities are visited by *Fram* on her positioning cruises to and from the Southern hemisphere; photographed in the Pool of London in April 2009. (John Bryant)

Qullissat, Greenland: *Fram*, ice floes, tenderboats and flowers, what more do you need? *(Andrea Klaussner/Hurtigruten)*

THE 2007 EXPEDITION SHIP

As far back as 2003, OVDS had been planning to build a ship specifically for wintertime service and summertime cruising around Greenland, a concept initiated by the company in 1998 with their 'explorer programme'. A NOK 530 million contract was signed with Fincantieri, the keel laying ceremony taking place on 21st August 2006 at their Monfalcone shipyard, near Trieste, Italy, with the ship being delivered to Hurtigruten , as scheduled, on 23rd April 2007.

The *Fram*, 11,647 gross tons, is named after Fridtjof Nansen's polar exploration vessel, the first to explore the seas around both the North and South Poles. The name was approved by the management of the Fram Museum in Oslo, Norway who also offered to contribute authentic expedition display pieces and information on the original *Fram*.

Registered in Narvik (but now Tromsø), the *Fram* has a reinforced hull for cruising in Arctic waters, is 114 metres in length with a beam of 20.2 metres. Her MAK6M25 diesels (total output 7,920 kW), give the ship a maximum speed of 16 knots. Within her eight decks are 136 high quality cabins and 39 suites with a total of 318 berths. The ship has a cargo capacity of 25 cars and 200 pallets of freight.

Facilities include an observation lounge, library, internet café, restaurant, bistro, sauna, Jacuzzi, a fitness centre, and two conference/lecture rooms with seating for up to 250 people. A specially designed tender deck makes passenger embarkation easy,

The locals peace and quiet is about to be disturbed as expedition guests disembark from the *Fram*. *(Eberhard Scharff/Hurtigruten)*

The photographer has cleverly used the ice floe to produce this beautiful image of *Fram*. *(Tomas Mauch/Hurtigruten)*

A lone sentinal keeps a close watch over *Fram* in Antarctica. *(Ingrid Gremler/Hurtigruten)*

ensuring that onshore expeditions are safe and comfortable.

The ship's interior very much reflects the culture and language of Greenland, with the public areas bearing Inuit words of symbolic meaning, for example; Qilak (sky/heaven) Lounge, Imaq (sea) Restaurant, Nunami (on land) Lobby. The furnishings feature extensive use of traditional Nordic materials of wool, leather and oak. Artworks from both Norwegian and Greenlandic artists are displayed throughout the ship.

The *Fram's* delivery voyage was more in the way of a four part cruise; sailing from Venice to Barcelona, by way of Dubrovnik, Naples, and Monte Carlo before calling at Cádiz, Lisbon, Rouen, and sailing through Tower Bridge to the Pool of London. The third leg took her to Rotterdam, Hamburg, Copenhagen and on to Oslo where on 19th May, the ship's Godmother, Crown Princess Mette Marit, formally named the ship.

Her summer programmes see her visiting the west and south-east coasts of Greenland, Iceland and circumnavigations of Svalbard. Greenland cruises are concentrated more on the west coast, with the focus on Disko Bay (Ilulissat). These experience cruises in polar waters are specifically aimed towards an active, broad and affluent international public with a generally wider spread of ages than is typical for the traditional Hurtigruten voyages. For 2018 she will extend these cruises to sail in the wake of the early explorers from Kangerlussuaq in Greenland to Cambridge Bay in Canada, and an

opportunity for guests to experience the raw and daunting beauty of that terrain. Even today, few ships have the *Fram's* capability to navigate this sea passage that cuts through the remote Arctic regions of North America.

Antarctica is still the most inaccessible of destinations but with the *Fram* travellers have been able experience it at close hand from November to March. Most of her voyages start from and finish at Ushuaia in Argentina with positioning runs from and to Buenos Aires. A variety of itineraries are on offer covering visits to the South Shetland Islands, the Antarctic Peninsular, the Falkland Islands and South Georgia.

The *Fram's* positional cruises, designed to make the transfer between the northern and southern hemispheres more interesting as well as profitable, are firmly established and now include the east coasts of North America. Her European cruises, in which her ports of call are varied each year, give special attention to important cultural history sites along the coastlines and are aimed at differing Hurtigruten markets, including the corporate sector. Her itineraries are now being extended to include the whole of the North American Eastern Seaboard, the Caribbean and Central America, Brazil's Amazon Basin, the whole of the east coast down to Montevideo in Uruguay and onto Antarctica before returning northwards along the west coast of Chile and Peru to explore the Lands of the Incas.

CHAPTER EIGHT

Momentous Change

NEW OWNERS

With 125 years of service behind it, the Coastal Express has seen well in excess of 80 ships on the route. Initially taken from Norwegian domestic trade or foreign routes, facilities were quite basic but eventually new ships were custom built to suit the ever-changing needs of the service. Today's fleet of modern multi-purpose vessels is designed with palletised loading, refrigerated compartments and hook ups, vehicle drive-on facilities and of course five star cruise liner standards.

Apart from providing a daily lifeline for the 34 communities served along the 1,352 nautical miles between Bergen and Kirkenes, the ships have always attracted a loyal following of round trip passengers. Hurtigruten is conscious that it has a mission and a duty which extends beyond merely bringing tourists to its destinations. Operating in some of the world's most vulnerable regions close to nature and the local culture through cooperation with its many tourist providers, the company is able to offer its guests experiences which nobody else can match.

Under the direction of Daniel Skjeldam, who took over as CEO of

Hurtigruten in 2012 the company became leaner and fitter without losing any of the essence that is Coastal Express. Moving its operations to Tromsø and with a fresh focus on the hotel and restaurant sectors, by 2013 it was experiencing more bookings and in consequence higher income streams. Fresh initiatives included sailing through Lyngenfjorden in April and May on the southbound leg towards Tromsø. Even the number of cancelled calls had been halved. As part of the restructuring by 2014 all the fleet had been re-registered in Tromsø.

In September 2014 the company announced that as from the summer of 2015 the ms *Nordstjernen,* having been sold to Vestland Rederi AS, Totvastad, Haugesund, in December 2012, would be returning to Hurtigruten service to supplement the *Fram's* sailings around Svalbard. Initially, in addition to the scheduled cruises for her new owners she would be offering 3-4 day cruises between June and September based on Longyearbyen. Her new Arctic adventures began with a positioning voyage from Bergen on June 1, via the Western Fjords of Norway to Alesund, Lofotens, Tromsø and Honningsvåg/North Cape before continuing to Svalbard. Such was

Today, the heritage ship ***Nordstjernen*** spends her summer months on charter to Hurtigruten with cruises around Svalbard. (*Trym Ivar Bergsmo/Hurtigruten*)

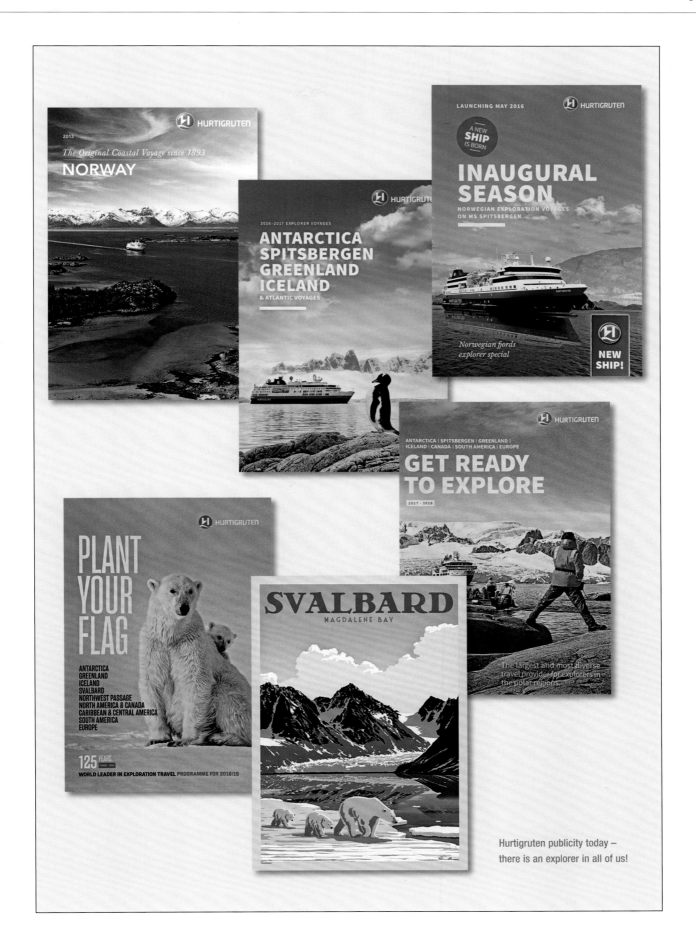

Hurtigruten publicity today –
there is an explorer in all of us!

The 2009 Portuguese built ferry *Atlântida* which became Hurtigruten's *Spitsbergen* in 2016. (Author's Collection)

Spitsbergen's Christening at Svolvær 6th July 2016 was performed by professional adventurer Cecile Skog. (Ørjan Bertelsen/Hurtigruten)

the demand for the *Nordstjernen's* cruises that for 2017 no less than thirty 6 day cruises were scheduled and that this pattern of sailings is to continue in both 2018 and 2019.

In late October it was announced that Trygve OBI, which owned 33.14% of Hurtigruten, was selling a stake of 28.14% to the joint venture company Silk Bidco AS Norway (90% owned by British buyout fund TDR Capital), leaving investors Trygve OBI and Petter Stordalen with 5% each. Whilst it would mean that the company would be in effect British owned, TDR Capital stressed that it would continue with Norwegian management in order to preserve its history and quality. They envisaged investing up to NOK 5.5 billion into the company geared towards expanding expedition experiences with the promise of up to four new ships to be constructed.

Perhaps, however, the most significant change in the organisation came internally in 2015 when the company moved from being a public limited company i.e. ASA (Allmennaksjeselskap) to a limited company and is now known as Hurtigruten AS (Aksjeselskap).

The first firm news of an expansion in the explorer programme came with an announcement in June 2015, that after modifications to make her more suited to explorer voyages, the *Midnatsol* would join the *Fram* in Antarctica for the 2016/17 season. The focus would be on polar science and nature with the ship carrying her own team of scientists together with a 'science laboratory' on board.

The answer to the question 'who would replace her in the winter months on the Coastal Voyage?' came with the news that the ms *Ferry Atlântida*, currently at the Navy Shipyards of the Arsenal do Alfeite, Almada near Lisbon, had been purchased. Built in 2009 as a passenger/car ferry for Atlântico Line at Viana do Castelo, north of Porto, for the Azores inter-island routes she had never entered service. The owners had cited deadweight issues (the specification was also changed during building) amongst their reasons for refusal.

All dressed up and ready to go! *Spitsbergen* at Bergen for the first time. (Tor Farstad/Hurtigruten)

An early morning arrival in the summer sunshine at Trondheim for *Spitsbergen*, July 2016. *(Uwe Jakob)*

Spitsbergen manoeuvring towards her berth at Trondheim, note the large duck tail at the stern which reduces wash and improves fuel efficiency
(Uwe Jakob)

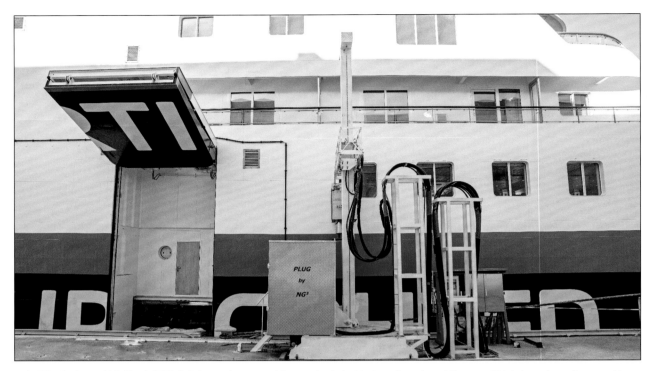

'Cold Ironing' - on 28th March 2018 *Spitsbergen* inaugurated the new land electrical supply system at Bergen, which helps reduce nitrogen oxide and carbon dioxide emissions from ships whilst in port. *(John Bryant)*

However, despite having lain idle for quite a while, Hurtigruten inspected and studied the ship for several months before deciding that at 97m in length with potentially good cabin capacity she was the exact type of ship that they needed. Whilst major work would need to be done to make her suitable for her new roles, in essence she would be a 'new' ship and the first for Hurtigruten for nearly ten years. She sailed from Portugal and arrived on 6th July 2015 at Öresundsvarvet, Landskrona, Sweden with the temporary name of *Norway Explorer* where a more in depth assessment was made.

Four months later to the day the *Norway Explorer* left Landskrona on 6th November 2015 arriving 3 days later at the Rissa (Fosen) yard, Trondheim for her conversion and refurbishment. The expectation was that she would be handed over to Hurtigruten as the *Spitsbergen* in the late spring of the following year.

At a structural level, the ship would undergo major surgery to ensure that she would be a modern and eco-friendly ship, reducing both emissions and fuel consumption. The bow of the ship had to be strengthened so that she could met the necessary DNV-FL 1C ice class certification needed for sailing in polar waters. Likewise the stern of the ship would be fitted with a large 'duck tail' to reduce wash as well as enhance fuel efficiency.

Tillberg Design of Sweden, one of the world's leading marine architecture and interior design companies, was contracted to be responsible for the interior refurbishment. They produced an

The Torget Restaurant on board *Spitsbergen*, Deck 5. *(Uwe Jakob)*

Spitsbergen's Explorer Lounge and Bar. *(Uwe Jakob)*

The spacious Panoramic Lounge is forward on **Spitsbergen**'s Deck 6. *(Uwe Jakob)*

outstanding fresh Scandinavian feel, with 'sea and fjord blue shades and whites from icy landscapes', modern and elegant throughout the ship. As part of their brief, as far as possible the materials used had to be of a natural origin, such as wood, slate and leather.

Her former garage on Deck 3 became the tender deck adapted to embark passengers on shore excursions, with her Polarcirkel (inflatable boats) located in the aft storage area. Forward on this level are the crew cabins and their lounge together with further storage and provision rooms. Above, Deck 4 is almost entirely given over to passenger cabins, housing also the laundry and ship's hospital (manned by a resident doctor and a nurse).

Moving upwards, Deck 5 houses the main passenger gangway which leads into the lobby and reception area. The Reception Desk is constantly manned and serves as the place to book tours and expeditions. The lobby has panoramic floor to ceiling windows, a seating area, the Internet Cafe corner (4 computers, 1 printer) together with a video games arcade (starboard). Next to the arcade is the Kids Playroom, which doubles as a nursery.

Forward is the main Explorer Panorama Lounge and Bar, which hosts daily multimedia presentations and professional lectures by the scientists and wildlife experts on board. The Bistro, midships on the portside, sells light snacks and drinks and is open 24 hours each day. The adjacent small shop sells Hurtigruten merchandise,

together with hand-made Norwegian souvenirs, toys and special occasion gifts. The aft-located restaurant is the ship's dining room for buffet style breakfast and lunch with dinner being waiter served.

Deck 6 (Promenade Deck) is given over to cabin accommodation except for the forward lounge and bar which is, in essence, an extension of the Explorer Lounge on Deck 5. The lounge's outdoor area is known as the Passenger Bridge being located right under the Navigation Bridge on Deck 7 with its narrow open promenade around the bow of the ship.

The final transformation of the *Atlântida* into the *Spitsbergen*, from a so-called Portuguese 'ugly duckling' into a Norwegian 'ice swan', took place on July 6th, 2016 under the midnight sun at Svolvær in the Lofotens with both the *Richard With* and *Midnatsol* in attendance. The choice of Cecile Skog as godmother to the ship was most apt given the varied explorer role the ship undertakes. Cecile Skog is a professional adventurer, tour guide and expert lecturer from Ålesund, most noted for being the only woman who has participated in expeditions to both the North and South Poles as well as being the only 'Seven Summits' woman in the world (i.e. has stood on top the highest mountain on each of the continents).

The *Spitsbergen* replaced the *Midnatsol* on the classic coastal route in the autumn of 2016 and continues to act as her winter replacement. During her first season of service the *Spitsbergen*

The new tender landing platform on the *Midnatsol*, at the time she was operating off Mikkelsen Harbour, Trinity Island, Antarctica. *(Karsten Bidstrup/Hurtigruten)*

Awesome Antarctica - *Midnatsol* off Neko Harbour. *(Andreas Kalvig Anderson/Hurtigruten)*

Since 2016 the 'new generation' ships have been subject to a major refurbishment; this is part of *Nordnorge* 's 'Torget' or Dining Square. *(Tor Farstad/Hurtigruten)*

suddenly found herself with a 'smelly' problem concerning the heated floors in the ensuite areas of the cabins. It transpired that the glue and mastic adhesives used between the heating cables and the tiles on the floor were reacting to the moisture and heat. Fosen Yards quickly found an anwer to the problem though it did mean that the ship was taken out of service for a complete 11 day round trip in March 2017 in order that the remedial work could be done as part of the ship's warranty with the shipyard.

For the summer months of 2017 the *Spitsbergen* introduced her own new explorer voyages via the Shetland and Faroe Islands, Iceland and Greenland. In a first for Hurtigruten she also sailed to Canada, cruising the Labrador and Baffin Island coastlines and onto Newfoundland to L'Anse aux Meadows, the first known Viking settlement in North America.

All of this new investment has been well worth it, as for example, in the UK Small Cruise Ship Awards for 2017 the *Spitsbergen* was awarded first place in no less than five categories (o*verall; cabin accommodation; service; shore excursions and value for money).* High praise indeed!

The *Midnatsol's* voyages which began in 2106-2017 took in not just Antarctica but also both most of the east and west coasts of South America, starting with Brazil's Amazon Basin and down the east coast to Montevideo in Uruguay. At the end of her Antarctic cruises she returned home northwards along the west coast of South America, via Chile and Peru exploring the Lands of the Incas. These latter cruises are scheduled to be in the hands of the *Fram* in 2018. Positioning cruises from to and from Bergen were also on offer including cultural visits to Spain and North Africa.

MORE UPGRADES TO THE FLEET

In addition to embarking on a programme to reduce ship emissions whilst in port by operating on shore power, in early September 2015 came the news that four of the 'new generation' ships would be getting a total internal makeover as from January 2016 as part of the new 'Arctic Interior' concept designed to increase capacity. This would take place at the Fosen (Rissa) Shipyard, near Trondheim where the *Spitsbergen* was currently undergoing her transformation. The ships had all been in service for around 20 years but the much loved cosy club atmosphere was beginning to show its age and in need of a facelift. Whilst the *Polarlys* was scheduled to be the first ship to be refurbished in the end it was the *Kong Harald*, followed by the *Polarlys, Nordkapp and Nordnorge.* Three shifts of workers worked around the clock with only 22 days allowed for each ship to be renovated. As with the *Spitsbergen*, the interiors of ships would be upgraded 'in a style where colours and materials are sourced from nature,' reinforcing the feeling of comfortable and enjoyable expedition travel. The results have transformed the ships into something contemporary and exciting,

Kong Harald - Expedition Suite. *(Ørjan Bertelsen/Hurtigruten)*

Kysten Fine Dining area - *Kong Harald*. *(Ørjan Bertelsen/Hurtigruten)*

more open and airy in plan, and should enable them to serve on the route for many more years to come. Guest satisfaction has been high and this refurbishment will be applied to more of the fleet.

Following on from this it was announced in late October 2017 that a NOK 400m secured bond loan had been agreed in order to repurchase the *Richard With* and *Nordlys* (from Kystruten, Oslo and Kirkberg Shipping AS, Bergen respectively) and partly finance their renovation in order to bring them into line with the rest of their 'new generation' fleetmates. These ships had been originally sold in December 2002 as a means of increasing capital when then then owners, OVDS and TFDS, were experiencing some financial constraints. Both vessels were then leased back as bare boats charters with the option to purchase after 10 or 15 years, which Hurtigruten AS have now excerised.

Nordnorge - Explorer Bar. *(Tor Farstad/Hurtigruten)*

Multe Bakery & Ice Cream Parlour - *Nordnorge*. *(Tor Farstad/Hurtigruten)*

Nordnorge - Panorama Lounge. *(John Bryant)*

A powerful view of the *Midnatsol* at anchor at
Paradise Harbour. *(Miles Cowsill)*

427

CHAPTER NINE
World Leader

In keeping with their aim to be the most environmentally sustainable means of travel along the Norwegian coastline and polar territories the company has put into action a number of initiatives to ensure that their ships leave the smallest footprint possible.

In early April 2016, it was announced that they were seeking ways of converting their vessels to battery-hybrid propulsion as part of this aim. The company had already embarked on a programme of reducing ship emissions whilst in port by operating on shore power, a process known as 'cold ironing'. The *Spitsbergen* became the first to use this technology at Bergen on 28th February 2018, where ships are berthed from between 5½ hours to 8 hours depending on the season. It is estimated that nitrogen oxide emissions will be reduced by 1,600 tonnes per year, with the CO_2 reduction even greater. The company is also working with engineers on various projects to enable vessels to sustain operation on battery power for two to four hours before switching to algae-based fuels until a recharging port can be reached.

Sailing in pristine environments comes with responsibility and it therefore came as no surprise when in April 2016 Hurtigruten formally announced an order for two new (with an option for two more) hybrid powered expedition ships with ice strengthened hulls

Hurtigruten CEO Daniel Skjeldam (right) and Kleven Yards, Ulsteinvik, CEO, Ståle Rasmussen (left) press the button to start the welding robots on the construction of *Roald Amundsen* – 24th February 2017. *(Marianne Hovden/Kleven/Hurtigruten)*

suited to working in polar ice conditions, scheduled for delivery in 2019. The vessels would be the world's most modern explorer ships, with the focus on maximum safety, comfort, fuel efficiency and environmental protection, enabling them to sail more quietly and cleanly than anything else before.

At that time Hurtigruten CEO Daniel Skjeldam said, *'It is exactly*

The shape of things to come in 2019 - *Roald Amundsen* and *Fridtjof Nansen*. *(Hurtigruten)*

105 years since Roald Amundsen became the first person in the world to plant his flag on the South Pole; 128 years since Fridtjof Nansen skied across Greenland; and 125 years since Richard With, Hurtigruten's founder, first started exploration tourism in the Arctic. What could be more natural and appropriate than to name our new ships after these inspiring trailblazers.'

The ships have been designed by Rolls-Royce, in collaboration with the highly respected Norwegian yacht designer Espen Øino, and would also in theory have the capability to operate on the classic service route along the Norwegian coast.

On 24th February 2017 construction officially started at the Kleven Shipyard, Ulsteinvik, south of Ålesund, which had previously built three of the current fleet, *Nordkapp*, *Nordnorge* and *Finnmarken*. Hurtigruten's CEO Daniel Skjeldam assisted by Kleven's CEO Ståle Rasmussen pressing the button to activate the welding robots to begin the fabrication of the steel section which will house the *Roald Amundsen's* revolutionary hybrid engines.

Other sections of the *Roald Amundsen* were built at the Montex Shipyard, Gdansk, Poland, partners in the Kleven Group who would also construct similar elements for the *Fridtjof Nansen*.

On 24th October 2017, the first hull segments of the *Roald Amundsen*, comprising the bow block, two bottom sections, the stern section (with aft overhang and transom) and a three-storey section of the superstructure including a wheelhouse, were dispatched on barge-pontoon and towed to the Kleven shipyard in Ulsteinvik arriving there on Thursday 2nd November. The bow section was immediately manouevred into place on the slipway in front of the main superstructure block, and as a result the *Roald Amundsen* was beginning to look more shiplike. Such is the pace at which ships are constructed today the *Roald Amundsen* took to the water at noon on 17th February 2018, fittingly to be greeted by the *Lofoten*, Hurtigruten's oldest member of the fleet which was on her northbound service.

The new hybrid battery technology on these two latest Hurtigruten exploration ships enables the ship to sail with electric propulsion for short periods of time, the main gain being a reduction in fuel consumption and reduced CO2 emissions by at least 20%.

Four Rolls-Royce Bergen B33:45 engines each with an output of 3,600kW used in combination with batteries are at the heart of the innovative hybrid solution onboard these two vessels. This technology for the *Roald Amundsen* and *Fridtjof Nansen* is planned for delivery in two phases. In phase one, auxiliary battery power will enable large reductions in fuel consumption and this is being installed installed for the first time on a cruise ship. For phase two, larger batteries will be installed, enabling fully electric sailing across longer distances and over longer periods of time. This could be used when while sailing into port and in vulnerable areas allowing silent and emission free sailing, Rolls-Royce aims to install this as soon as

Roald Amundsen begins to look more like a ship at the Kleven Shipyard, Ulsteinvik, November 2017. *(Tor Arne Aasen/Samferdselsfoto)*

A superb aerial view of a snowy Kleven Shipyard, Ulsteinvik with *Roald Amundsen* under construction, 30th November 2017. *(Per Eide)*

Launch day for *Roald Amundsen*, 17th February 2018. *(Oclin/Hurtigruten)*

Another stunning aerial view of *Roald Amundsen* under construction at the Kleven Shipyard, Ulsteinvik. *(Per Eide)*

Roald Amundsen is greeted by Hurtigruten's *Lofoten* which had diverted from her schedule to witness the launching at Ulsteinvik. *(Tor Arne Aasen/Samferdselsfoto)*

the technology is ready, firstly in the *Fridtjof Nansen* and then in the *Roald Amundsen*. Hurtigruten are of the opinion that the future of shipping is for silent and emission free operation and are using their new expedition ships as groundbreakers to show the world that hybrid propulsion on large ships is possible and particularly pertinent when sailing in the Arctic and Antarctic.

With the *Roald Amundsen* and *Fridtjof Nansen*, Hurtigruten are setting new standards in interior design, mirroring the breath-taking waters and landscapes where the expedition ships sail. Materials are predominantly Norwegian, inspired by nature, in a Scandinavian style approach in the use of granite, oak and birch, and wool amongst other mediums.

On board Deck 3 is the Expedition Launch where guests embark on excursions and where the Explorer Boats are stored. The Pharmacy and Medical Centre is also to be found on this deck. Decks 4 (on which the main passenger gangway is located) and Deck 5 are given over to cabin accommodation.

Deck 6 is the main passenger deck, where Aune, the main dining room, and the international kitchen Fredheim Restaurant can be found aft. Moving forward to the midships area where the Reception Centre and Shop are sited. Towards the bow is the Amundsen Science Center, where with the help of the ship's expedition team, guests are able to explore in hi-tech detail the places they are visiting. This facility also includes areas for photography, science, lectures and a library. A two level indoor/outdoor Observation Deck is wrapped around the bow and is and is one of several large

One of the Expedition Suites planned for *Roald Amundsen* and *Fridtjof Nansen*. *(Tillberg Design/Hurtigruten)*

An Arctic Superior Cabin, there will be no inside cabins on board either *Roald Amundsen* or *Fridtjof Nansen*. *(Tillberg Design/Hurtigruten)*

observation platforms on the ship which enable guests to get up-close to nature and wildlife.

At the bow on Deck 7 is the open Observation Deck, whilst midships is the Gym and Wellness Room. The remainder of this deck, together with the whole of Deck 8, is given over to cabin accomodation. Deck 9, in addition to more cabin accommodation, is the location for a third eating option, the fine dining Lindstrøm Restaurant. The Explorer Lounge is to be found on Deck 10 along with the heated Outdoor Infinity Pool, Jacuzzis and Panoramic Sauna. Finally, on Deck 11 is the open Explorer Deck which offers guests outstanding views of nature and wildlife.

CABIN ACCOMMODATION

Every cabin is outside facing, a first for Hurtigruten, with large windows which enable guests to immerse themselves in the breathtaking views outside. The accommodation is divided into three major categories, namely Expedition Suites, Arctic Superior and Polar Outside.

Expedition Suites are exclusively in upper and mid deck locations and are large, well-appointed for two to four guests, expansive windows with most having balconies. Some even have a private outside Jacuzzi. The suites feature flexible sleeping arrangements with comfortable sofas, sitting areas and TV, expresso maker and more.

Arctic Superior are comfortable and roomy and again can accommodate two to four guests. Those on the higher decks have balconies. Sleeping arrangements are flexible, with sofa beds, TV, tea and coffee making facilities etc, which makes this grade a popular choice. The Arctic Superior concept includes an amenity kit, kettle, tea and coffee.

The Polar Outside are primarily on the middle decks with

The Open Deck and Infinity Pool - *Roald Amundsen/Fridtjof Nansen.* *(Hurtigruten)*

The Aune dining area - *Roald Amundsen/Fridtjof Nansen.* *(Tillberg Design/Hurtigruten)*

Fredheim Restaurant - 'the international kitchen' - *Roald Amundsen/Fridtjof Nansen.* *(Tillberg Design/Hurtigruten)*

The Forward Explorer Lounge and Bar - *Roald Amundsen* and *Fridtjof Nansen*. *(Hurtigruten)*

windows, and can also accommodate two to four guests. Most are spacious, with flexible sleeping arrangements, TV and offer an excellent standard of accommodation.

THE FIRST SEASON

For her first season in 2019 the *Roald Amundsen* will cruise along the Norwegian Coastline on a series of 14 day tours to and from Hamburg based on the Bergen-Kirkenes route which Hurtigruten has operated since 1893Among the planned new destinations the hybrid ships will visit are Reine, Rosendal, Sommarøy and Skarsvåg, the latter being the world's most northerly fishing village.

And it doesn't stop there as in addition to the *Fram* exploring parts of Canada's North West Passage, 2019 will see the *Roald Amundsen* tackle the whole of the route. Hurtigruten will be the first company in the world to sail this route using battery packs and hybrid propulsion, more than 100 years after Roald Amundsen, the explorer, became the first person to sail through the famous and notorious passage from the Atlantic Ocean to the Pacific in his polar boat *Gjøa*. But where it took Amundsen three years to achieve, the

Hurtigruten ship will take three weeks, from Greenland and the Atlantic Ocean to the east, to Nome and the Pacific Ocean before finally sailing southwards along Canada's famous 'inside passage' to Vancouver.

Not to be outdone, the *Spitsbergen* will expand the exploration options to the east with late summer sailings from Tromsø to Murmansk and Frans Josef Land, the latter one of the world's most

Part of the Amundsen Science Center on board *Roald Amundsen* *(Hurtigruten)*

A side profile impression of the new hybrid explorer ships. *(Hurtigruten)*

Explorer Lounge - *Roald Amundsen* and *Fridtjof Nansen. (Hurtigruten)*

spectacular, yet at least visited destinations. Breathtaking experiences indeed!

With its unique heritage, highly skilled crews and modern purpose built ships on all the routes they serve, Hurtigruten continues to offer awe-inspiring experiences that no one else can match.

POSTSCRIPT
A NEW CONTRACT (2021-2031)

In September 2017 the Norwegian Government outlined the tender requirements for the next contract on the Kystruten Bergen-Kirkenes (Coastal Express) route to run from 2021 to 2031. They wished for increased competition on the route which they proposed

An impression of *Roald Amundsen* cruising in the beautiful Kirkefjord, Lofotens. *(Hurtigruten)*

might be best achieved by sharing it between two or three shipping companies. This would take the form of three packages; two would involve companies providing four ships, whilst the third would require a three ship operation. Each package would be for continuous service throughout the year from Bergen to Kirkenes, with all ports on the route to be served daily as before. Any vessels used on the route would be required to have the same capacity as today, both for both freight and passenger traffic.

The contract would be awarded to suppliers on the basis of the lowest price offered subject to meeting all the new environmental requirements (e.g. lowering CO_2 emissions from shipping by at least 25%). A single company could be awarded all three contracts which would be for 10 years with an option to extend by one year.

In the event, on 23rd March 2018 Hurtigruten was awarded the major tranche of the new contract. This brought much relief and pleasure not just to the company but from their many clients (service providers, businesses, port to port travellers and loyal cruise guests) built up over the years. As part of the contract Hurtigruten will convert their vessels to LNG (Liqiuid Natural Gas) and battery operation. (Rolls-Royce have won a billion NOK contract to convert up to nine of the Hurtigruten fleet). On the days when Hurtigruten is not operating on the Norwegian coastal (Kystruten) service their three 'millennium class' ships (*Finnmarken*, *Trollfjord* and *Midnatsol*) will, in a separate commercial venture, sail along the same coastline between Bergen and Kirkenes carrying cruise only guests to selected ports in a new phase of cruise tourism offering further explorer opportunities.

The remainder of the contract was awarded to Per Sævik's

An artist's impression of the four new ships Havila Kystruten will build to serve on the coastal route as from 2021. *(Havila)*

Havila Kystruten, a newly formed subsidiary of Havila Holding AS (based at Fosnavåg, Sunnmøre, near Ulsteinvik). He has interests in the offshore oil supply industry, in fishing and is the majority shareholder in Fjord 1, one of the largest local ferry operators in Norway. Four new ships are to be built, designed by Havyard Design AS which is owned by the Sævik family, and will be eco friendly, using both natural gas (LNG) and battery hybrid propulsion. Each will measure around 125m in length and have the capacity to accommodate up to 700 people.

Long regarded as one of Norway's 'jewels in the crown' and with an unmatched legacy of great service behind it the coastal route will no doubt continue to evolve as needs change.

In the meantime 125 years of the 'most beautiful voyage in the world' is something more than well worth celebrating!

Midnatsol powering her way past the Lofoten Wall towards Stamsund en route from Svolvær. *(John Bryant)*

The Coastal Express Companies 1893-2020

Vesteraalens Dampskibsselskab AS (VDS) 1893 – 1987

This company was founded on the initiative of Richard With based at Stockmarnes, Vesterålen on 10th November 1881. That same year, the shipping company's first ship, *Vesteraalen* (*ex Arendal* 1865), was purchased from Arendals Dampskibsselskab and went into regular service between Senja, Vesterålen, Lofoten and Bergen. It was not until the establishment of the Coastal Express that VDS became one of the major players on the 'long coast' of Norway. In 1985 Ofotens Dampskibsselskap secured a majority stake in the company, and at the end of 1987/88 the company formally merged into Ofotens and Vesteraalens Dampskibsselskap (OVDS).

Det Bergen Dampskibsselskab AS (BDS) 1894 – 1979

BDS was formed on 12th December 1851 to operate regular shipping services between Bergen and Hamburg. The company soon expanded with routes to the England, France and Iceland and later ventured into cruise liners. The distinctive black company funnel with its three white rings became well known across the shipping world. From the 1920's to the late 1960's the company had 2,500 employees and a fleet of 30-40 ships, however, the 1970's were more difficult. In 1979 their four ships were sold to TFDS (see below). In November 1984, the company was taken over by AS Kosmos in Sandefjord later being sold on to RoNoTro AS in December 1988, at which point the company lost any individual identity.

Det Nordenfjeldske Dampskibsselskab AS (NFDS) 1895 – 1989

NFDS came into being on 28th January 1857 to provide a regular shipping service from Trondheim to Hamburg and Newcastle. NFDS had a close association with BDS and in addition to the Coastal Express were involved in international routes to the Mediterranean as well as later on with tankers and cruise ships. In 1984 Norcem acquired a majority share and within a year the company had been sold on to AS Kosmos who had also acquired BDS. The same fate awaited NFDS when their ships were transferred to TFDS in August 1989.

Det Stavangerske Dampskibsselskab (DSD) AS 1919 – 1979

Founded on 12th February 1855, DSD began to develop services from Stavanger to Bergen, Oslo, Kristiansand and Frederikshavn

Polarlys' funnel is very much a 'one off' when compared to her sister 'new generation' vessels. (*John Bryant*)

(Denmark). In 1919 they joined the consortium, extending the service to Stavanger, but this only lasted until 1936. Their vessels remained on the route and it was not until 1978 that they sold their last remaining ship *ms Kong Olav* to VDS and as a result ceased to be part of the Coastal Express. Today, the company is still very much in business being a major shareholder in both Norled AS (operating car ferry and fast craft services) and Nor Lines (coastal cargo).

Ofotens Dampskibsselskab (ODS) AS 1936 – 1987

Ofotens Dampskibsselskab AS was founded on 24th July 1912 to carry traffic in the Ofotfjorden (Narvik) area. The company later started an express Trondheim-Narvik service in 1924, whilst also extending local routes. From 1st November 1936, ODS became part of the Hurtigruten with Narvik having its own weekly calls. From the mid 1980's there was a rapid expansion of assets, culminating in the acquisition of Vesteraalens Dampskibsselskab (VDS). The new company was renamed Ofotens Vesteraalens Dampskibsselskab (OVDS) but retained the ODS logo.

Det Nordlandske Dampskipsselskap (NDS) AS 1945 – 1958

The company came into being on 13th August 1927 when it introduced the *Skjerstad* from Salten Dampskibsselskab onto the Saltdal-Bodø-Trondheim service; a move which caused friction with both BDS and NFDS, a situation which wasn't resolved until 1936. After the Second World War in autumn 1945, the company became a member of the Hurtigruten using a replacement *Skjerstad* which underwent a major refit. However, in 1958 they forfeited their place on the Coastal Express as they were not able to provide more modern tonnage for the route.

Troms Fylkes Dampskibsselskap (TFDS) AS 1979 – 2006

TFDS's ancestry dates from 1866 with its involvement in the coastal trade around Troms. Over the years the company built up an extensive route network, the name became modernized into the present form in 1925. Through various mergers and acquisitions, particularly of the BDS and NFDS fleet in 1979 and 1989, TFDS became one of just two operators managing the Coastal Express. Based in Tromsø the company has also operated a number of car ferries and passenger ferries, primarily in the Troms area. Listed on the Oslo Stock Exchange until 2006 when it merged with Ofotens og Vesteraalens Dampskibsselskab to create the Hurtigruten Group.

Ofotens Vesteraalens Dampskibsselskab (OVDS) AS 1987 – 2006

After Ofotens took a majority stake in VDS in 1985, the two

A rear view of *Nordlys'* funnel in the TFDS livery she had up to 2006. *(Franz Clemens)*

companies formally merged in January 1988 together with some of the regional ferry operators become OVDS. The new company became a major force operating six ships, as well as having interests in tourism and international cruising. OVDS's main office was in Narvik while the ferry section was located in Stokmarknes. The company merged with Troms Fylkes Dampskibsselskap in 2006 to form Hurtigruten ASA. At the time of the merger the company had about 1,500 employees and operated 14 ships, 18 car ferries and 14 fast passenger ferries.

Finnmark Fylkesrederi og Rutelskap (FFR) 1988 – 1996

Finmarkens Amtsrederi was founded in 1916 to take over local ferry routes that had previously been run under contract from the government. The name was later changed to Finnmark Fylkesrederi og Rutelskap as the company extended its activities to bus services and in particular tourist traffic to North Cape. In the autumn of 1988 the company became part of the Hurigruten set up but this ceased when the *Lofoten* was resold to OVDS in 1996. FFR's responsibilities for local bus routes and ferry routes in Finnmark are now under the management of Boreal Transport Norge AS.

Hurtigruten AS 2006 - present

Hurtigruten ASA was the result of the long-awaited merger on 1st March 2006 between Troms Fylkes Dampskibsselskap (TFDS) and Ofotens og Vesteraalens Dampskibsselskab (OVDS), although the name did not formally change until 26th April 2007. In 2013 the company moved its headquarters from Narvik to Tromsø. In 2015 the company moved from being a public limited company i.e. ASA (Allmennaksjeselskap) to a limited company and is now known as Hurtigruten AS (Aksjeselskap).

Above: A fine image of **Polarlys** entering the harbour at Bodø. *(Uwe Jakob)*

Below: Looking majestic, **Nordnorge** at speed off Hjelmsøya on her way to Hammerfest from Havøysund. *(Miles Cowsill)*

Hurtigruten 125 Fleet

Lofoten

Call Sign:	LIXN
Built:	1964 - Akers Mek, Oslo
Hurtigruten Service:	1964 - present day
Gross Tonnage:	2,597
Dimensions:	286.8' x 43.6' x 22.0' (87.4m x 13.2m x 6.7m)
Passengers:	400
Machinery:	3,325 bhp, 7-cylinder DM 742 VT 2BF-90 B&W diesel
Service Speed:	15 knots
Car Capacity:	0

Vesterålen

Call Sign:	LLZY
Built:	1983 - Kaarbøs Mek, Harstad
Hurtigruten Service:	1983 - present day
Gross Tonnage:	4,072 (6,261 as from 1989)
Dimensions:	108.6m x 16.5m x 4.7m
Passengers:	554
Machinery:	2 x 3,200 bhp 16-cylinder 4T KVM-16 Bergen diesels
Service Speed:	15 knots
Car Capacity:	24

Kong Harald

Call Sign:	LGIY
Built:	1993 - Volkswerft, Stralsund, Germany
Hurtigruten Service:	1993 - present day
Gross Tonnage:	11,204
Dimensions:	121.8m x 19.2m x 4.7m
Passengers:	509
Machinery:	2 x 6,120 bhp 6-cylinder 4T Krupp MaK DM 6 M552 C diesels
Service Speed:	15 knots
Car Capacity:	22

Richard With

Call Sign:	LGWH
Built:	1993 - Volkswerft, Stralsund, Germany
Hurtigruten Service:	1993 - present day
Gross Tonnage:	11,204
Dimensions:	121.8m x 19.2m x 4.7m
Passengers:	590
Machinery:	2 x 6,120 bhp 6-cylinder 4T Krupp MaK DM 6 M552 C diesels
Service Speed:	15 knots
Car Capacity:	22

Trollfjord arriving at Bergen at the end of another 11 day classic round voyage to Kirkenes. *(Miles Cowsill)*

Nordlys

Call Sign: LHCW
Built: 1994 - Volkswerft, Stralsund, Germany
Hurtigruten Service: 1993 - present day
Gross Tonnage: 11,204
Dimensions: 121.8m x 19.2m x 4.7m
Passengers: 590
Machinery: 2 x 6,120 bhp 6-cylinder 4T Krupp MaK DM 6 M552 C diesels
Service Speed: 15 knots
Car Capacity: 24

Nordkapp

Call Sign: JWPE3
Built: 1996 - Kværner Kleven, Ulsteinvik
Hurtigruten Service: 1996 - present day
Gross Tonnage: 11,386
Dimensions: 123.3m x 19.5m x 4.7m
Passengers: 590
Machinery: 2 x 6,120 bhp Krupp MaK DM 6M 552C diesels
Service Speed: 15 knots
Car Capacity: 24

Polarlys

Call Sign: LYHG
Built: 1996 - Ulstein Verft, Ulsteinvik
Hurtigruten Service: 1996 - present day
Gross Tonnage: 11,341
Dimensions: 123.0m x 19.5m x 7.2m
Passengers: 619
Machinery: 10, 800 bhp: 2 x Bergen BRM 9 diesels + 2 x Bergen KRG 9 diesels
Service Speed: 15 knots
Car Capacity: 26

Nordnorge

Call Sign: JWPC3
Built: 1997 - Kværner Kleven, Ulsteinvik
Hurtigruten Service: 1997 - present day
Gross Tonnage: 11,384
Dimensions: 123.3m x 19.5m x 4.7m
Passengers: 590
Machinery: 2 x 6,120 bhp Krupp MaK DM 6M 552C diesels
Service Speed: 15 knots
Car Capacity: 32

Finnmarken

Call Sign: LLRY
Built: 2002 - Kværner Kleven, Ulsteinvik
Hurtigruten Service: 2002 - present day
Gross Tonnage: 15,530
Dimensions: 138.5m x 21.5m x 5.0m
Passengers: 1,000
Machinery: 8,820 bhp: 2 x 4T DM Wartsila W 9L 32 + 2 x Wartsila W 6L 32 diesels
Service Speed: 15 knots
Car Capacity: 35

Trollfjord

Call Sign: LLVT
Built: 2002 - Fosen Mek, Rissa, near Trondheim
Hurtigruten Service: 2002 - present day
Gross Tonnage: 16,140
Dimensions: 135.8m x 21.5m x 5.1m
Passengers: 822
Machinery: 2 x 5,630 bhp 9-cylinder 4T DM W 9L 32 Wartsila diesels
Service Speed: 15 knots
Car Capacity: 35

Midnatsol (IV)

Call Sign: LMDH
Built: 2003 - Fosen Mek, Rissa, near Trondheim
Hurtigruten Service: 2003 - present day
Gross Tonnage: 16,151
Dimensions: 135.8m x 21.5m x 5.1m
Passengers: 970
Machinery: 2 x 5,630 bhp 9-cylinder 4T DM W 9L 32 Wartsila diesels
Service Speed: 15 knots
Car Capacity: 32

Fram

Call Sign: LADA7
Built: 2007 - Fincantieri, Trieste
Hurtigruten Service: 2007 - present day
Gross Tonnage: 11,647
Dimensions: 114.0m x 20.2m x 5.1m
Passengers: 318
Machinery: 7,920 kW: 2 x MAK6M25 diesels
Service Speed: 15 knots
Car Capacity: 0 (not used)

Spitsbergen

Call Sign:	LEIF
Built:	2009 - Arsenal do Alfeite, Almada; rebuilt 2015/2016 Fosen, Rissa
Hurtigruten Service:	2016 - present
Gross Tonnage:	7,025
Dimensions:	97.5m x 18.0m x 5.0m
Passengers:	335
Machinery:	11,200kW: 4 x ABC diesels
Service Speed:	17.4 knots
Car Capacity:	0

Roald Amundsen

Call Sign:	
Built:	2019 - Kleven Verft, Ulsteinvik
Hurtigruten Service:	2019 - present
Gross Tonnage:	20,889
Dimensions:	140m x 23.6m x 5.3m
Passengers:	530
Machinery:	Rolls-Royce: 4 x Bergen B33:45 engines
Service Speed:	15 knots
Car Capacity:	

Fridjtof Nansen

Call Sign:	
Built:	2019 - Kleven Verft, Ulsteinvik
Hurtigruten Service:	2019 - present
Gross Tonnage:	20,889
Dimensions:	140m x 23.6m x 5.3m
Passengers:	530
Machinery:	Rolls-Royce: 4 x Bergen B33:45 engines
Service Speed:	15 knots
Car Capacity:	

Nordstjernen (on charter)

Call Sign:	LATU
Built:	1956 - Blöhm & Voss, Hamburg
Hurtigruten Service:	1956 – 2012; 2015 – present
Gross Tonnage:	2,194
Dimensions:	80.7m x 12.6m x 6.1m
Passengers:	290
Machinery:	3,000 bhp 6-cylinder 2T B&W DM diesel
Service Speed:	15 knots
Car Capacity:	0

Spitsbergen departing Trondheim, the Explorer Deck above her bridge is a great viewing platform. *(Uwe Jakob)*

Index